10 Simple Solutions for Building Self-Esteem *is a very interesting and rewarding book! Clearly and warmly written, Schiraldi's book is filled with valuable and varied possibilities for enhancing self-esteem and exploring the wonder and mystery of this human life.*

> —Jeffrey Brantley, MD, founder and director of the Mindfulness-Based Stress Reduction Program at the Duke University Center for Integrative Medicine, author of *Calming Your Anxious Mind*, and coauthor of *The Dialectical Behavior Therapy Skills Workbook* and *Five Good Minutes*

Schiraldi skillfully blends theory and practice into a how-to manual for developing and strengthening self-esteem. Written in an easy, conversational style, this engaging book provides practical suggestions interspersed with real-life scenes.

> —A. Dean Byrd, Ph.D., MBA, MPH, president of Thrasher Research Fund and clinical professor at the University of Utah School of Medicine, and Elaine H. Byrd, Ed. D., professor of education at Utah Valley State College

Only rarely are we fortunate enough to encounter a teacher whose approach to examining life is powerful enough to change the negative assumptions that we hold about ourselves into positive ones. Such a teacher is Glenn Schiraldi. As his department chair, dean, and colleague in a major university, I have witnessed these changes over a period spanning three decades. Read this book if you want to try something that really works!

> —John Burt, Ph.D., professor of psychology at the University of Maryland

10 Simple Solutions for Building Self-Esteem

How to End Self-Doubt, Gain Confidence & Create a Positive Self-Image

GLENN R. SCHIRALDI, PH.D.

New Harbinger Publications, Inc.

Publisher's Note

This publication is designed to provide accurate and authoritative information in regard to the subject matter covered. It is sold with the understanding that the publisher is not engaged in rendering psychological, financial, legal, or other professional services. If expert assistance or counseling is needed, the services of a competent professional should be sought.

Body Appreciation Meditation in chapter 7: Condensed slightly and reprinted with permission from Canfield, Jack, (1985), "Body Appreciation," in *Wisdom, Purpose and Love*. Copyright 1985, Jack Canfield, coauthor, *Chicken Soup for the Soul* series. Do not reproduce without written permission. This version was originally reprinted with permission in Schiraldi, G. R. (2001). *The Self-Esteem Workbook*. Oakland, CA: New Harbinger Publications.

The defusing exercises "Identify the source of the Pain," "Milk, Milk, Milk," "Keep a Journal," and "Carry It With You" in chapter 3 is adapted with permission from *Get Out of Your Mind and Into Your Life* by S.C. Hayes and S. Smith, published by New Harbinger Publications, Oakland, CA in 2005. © by S.C. Hayes and S. Smith, 2005.

The "Candle of Forgiveness" exercise in chapter 9 is adapted with permission from *Act on Life Not on Anger* by G.H. Eifert, M. McKay, and J.P. Forsyth, published by New Harbinger Publications, Oakland, CA in 2006. © by G.H. Eifert, M. McKay, and J. P. Forsyth, 2006.

Raisin Exercise, Mindful Breathing, and Body Scan adapted from FULL CATASTROPHE LIVING by Jon Kabat-Zinn, copyright © 1990 by Jon Kabat-Zinn. Used by permission of Dell Publishing, a division of Random House, Inc.

The "Parable of the Broken Microscope Slides" in chapter 9 is adapted with permission from an unpublished sermon by the Rev. P.C. Shupe. © by P.C. Shupe 2006.

Distributed in Canada by Raincoast Books
All Rights Reserved
Printed in the United States of America

Copyright © 2007 by Glenn Schiraldi
New Harbinger Publications, Inc.
5674 Shattuck Avenue
Oakland, CA 94609
www.newharbinger.com

FSC
MIX
Paper
FSC® C011935

Acquired by Tesilya Hanauer; Cover design by Amy Shoup;
Edited by Karen O'Donnell Stein; Text design by Tracy Carlson

Library of Congress Cataloging-in-Publication Data

Schiraldi, Glenn R., 1947-

10 simple solutions for building self-esteem : how to end self-doubt, gain confidence, and create a positive self-image / Glenn Schiraldi.

p. cm.

ISBN-13: 978-1-57224-495-5

ISBN-10: 1-57224-495-X

1. Self-esteem. I. Title. II. Title: Ten simple solutions for building self-esteem.

BF697.5.S46S34 2007

158.1--dc22

2007012998

14 13 12

15 14 13 12 11 10 9

Contents

Acknowledgments

I n this book I have tried to combine the best of Western and Eastern psychology. I am grateful indeed for the pioneering work of Drs. Aaron Beck and Albert Ellis, who developed systematic ways to uproot destructive thought patterns, and to Dr. Jon Kabat-Zinn for developing the Mindfulness-Based Stress Reduction program, which has enabled mindfulness meditation practices to be applied to the alleviation of a host of medical and psychological conditions. Drs. Zindel Segal, Mark Williams, John Teasdale, and John McQuaid, as well as Paula Carmona, have brought together mindfulness practices and cognitive restructuring for the treatment of depression, while Dr. Jeffrey Brantley has applied mindfulness to the treatment of anxiety. I am thankful for the work of Dr. Steven Hayes, whose acceptance and commitment therapy, itself a skillful blending of West and East, has contributed much to this book. Mother Teresa, the Dalai Lama, Sogyal Rinpoche, Viktor Frankl, and many other extraordinary people have, through their example and teachings, also influenced this book greatly.

I deeply appreciate the students of all ages at the University of Maryland for so diligently and graciously experimenting with the practices in this book over the years, thereby helping me to better understand how to teach these practices more effectively.

Finally, I thank the wonderful, diligent people at New Harbinger Publications, especially Tesilya Hanauer, Heather Mitchener, and Karen O'Donnell Stein, the editors who have worked so thoughtfully with me to bring this book to fruition, and Tracy Carlson, who skillfully put my words into visual form.

Parts of this book are adapted from an earlier book of mine, *The Self-Esteem Workbook* (Schiraldi 2001).

Introduction

Why build self-esteem? The benefits of having self-esteem are numerous. Self-esteem is strongly associated with happiness, psychological resilience, and a motivation to live a productive and healthy life. Those lacking self-esteem are more likely to experience depression, anxiety, problem anger, chronic pain, immunosuppression, and a variety of other distressing physical and psychological symptoms. Indeed, Morris Rosenberg, Ph.D., the foremost researcher on self-esteem, said it well when he stated that nothing can be more stressful than the experience of lacking the basic anchor and security of a wholesome sense of self-worth. So self-esteem is essential to our health, coping abilities, survival, and sense of well-being.

During my tenure at the University of Maryland, I developed a skills-based course that improved self-esteem while reducing symptoms of depression, anxiety, and problem anger in adults eighteen to sixty-eight years of age (Schiraldi and Brown 2001). It was very good news to discover that mental health could be improved by employing such an approach. Those self-esteem skills are described in detail in my earlier book, *The Self-Esteem Workbook* (Schiraldi 2001), which you might someday find beneficial to tackle. However, if you now lack the time or readiness, or if current circumstances prevent you from beginning that systematic approach, then *10 Simple Solutions to Self-Esteem* is for you. It offers a simpler, quicker approach to increasing self-esteem—one that I hope you will find richly rewarding.

1

Know What Self-Esteem Is

M any myths and misunderstandings surround self-esteem. So let's begin by clearly understanding where we are going in this book. Self-esteem is a realistic, appreciative opinion of oneself. *Realistic* means we are dealing in the truth, being accurately and honestly aware of our strengths, weaknesses, and everything in between. *Appreciative*, however, suggests that we have good feelings overall about the person we see. Think of a friend who knows you well and cherishes you, recognizing that there is more to you than your faults, and you'll get a sense of what appreciative means.

Wholesome self-esteem is the conviction that one is as worthwhile as anyone else, but not more so. On one hand, we feel a quiet gladness to be who we are and a sense of dignity that comes from realizing that we share what all humans possess—intrinsic worth. On the other hand, those with self-esteem remain humble, realizing that everyone has much to learn and that we are all really in the same boat. There is no need to be arrogant or boastful, no need to think that we are more worthwhile as a person than others or more skilled or important than we really are.

Self-esteem is not the same as being self-centered, self-absorbed, or selfish. One who feels whole and secure in him- or herself is freer to be selfless. Can a criminal have high self-esteem? I suppose it is theoretically possible. However, a recent study found that aggressive, rebellious children were more likely to have been bullied; feel rejected, unhappy, and unloved; and have a poor self-image than less aggressive children (Sprott and Doob 2000). So it is important to distinguish the outer appearance of confidence from the quiet, steady, inner gladness that characterizes self-esteem.

Self-esteem is also not complacency or overconfidence, both of which can set us up for failure. Indeed, self-esteem is a strong motivator to work hard. And self-esteem is not just important for people in Western cultures; studies have shown that self-esteem is related to the mental health and happiness of adults in diverse cultures, including Asian (Lee 2002; Zhang 2005) and Middle Eastern societies (Hobfoll and London 1986; Hobfoll and Leiberman 1987).

The Building Blocks of Self-Esteem

Self-esteem rests upon three important factors, or building blocks. The first two blocks, unconditional worth and unconditional love, comprise the secure foundation for the third building block, growth. Generally, growth proceeds more effectively once the first two blocks are securely in place.

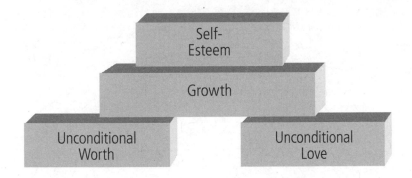

Figure 1

BUILDING BLOCK 1: UNCONDITIONAL WORTH

A basic premise is that all people have equal, immeasurable, unchanging intrinsic worth *as a person*. Worth as a person is neither earned nor increased or diminished by external factors, such as the way people treat you, bad decisions, or fluctuations in your bank account balance. Granted, this is not the message one hears in the marketplace or in certain social circles, which assign worth based on social or financial status, but the assumption of equal worth as a person is not a new one, and it can be quite empowering. Even very bright people may struggle with this concept, since they have been given the message that inner worth can rise or fall with performance or circumstances. So I've found that the following analogy helps. Perhaps you can visualize a spherical crystal, whose facets refract light so beautifully.

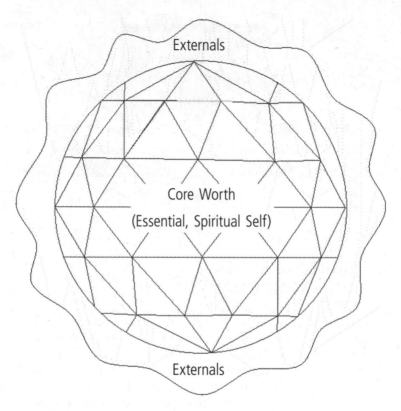

Figure 2   The Core Self

The crystal represents the core worth of each individual. Each facet of the crystal represents an attribute needed for living well. The facets include the capacities to love, think rationally, sacrifice, persevere, beautify and experience beauty, and make good decisions. Each facet may be polished and refined as we develop.

The core self might also be likened to a seed. Think of a newborn baby. Like that seed, the baby is already whole, possessing in embryo every attribute needed in order to flourish. The baby is *complete*, yet certainly not *completed* (that is, not perfect or fully developed).

Externals

Externals are outer events or circumstances that can alter the way we experience our worth but do not change our worth. Certain externals or experiences can camouflage or hide one's core worth, like a dark cloud or haze that surrounds and obscures it. Perhaps one has been emotionally, physically, or sexually abused. Such treatment by others can lead one to *believe* that one is defective at the core, even though the core remains whole and worthwhile. Similarly, people who have experienced trauma such as rape or combat often feel shattered inside, but they can benefit from the help of specially trained trauma counselors to again feel whole, or healed. (Interestingly, the words *whole*, *heal*, and *health* all derive from the same root. Please see the Recommended Resources section at the back of the book for suggestions regarding how to locate help.) Other externals act like sunlight, illuminating our core worth and helping us to experience that worth with satisfaction. For instance, being loved by others or successfully completing an important task helps us experience our worth more intensely, which feels good.

However, externals—whether good or bad—are not the core. If a person equates his or her core human worth to the value of his or her investment portfolio (an external), then that person's self-esteem will rise and fall with the stock market, going up and down like a roller coaster. Our goal in this chapter is to learn to separate core worth from externals. Imagine that the cloud around the crystal (core worth) is separated from the crystal and moved away from it, representing the fact that core worth is independent of externals.

Externals include the state of one's body (appearance, vitality, and health), economic status, gender, race, age, job title, promotions, awards, adversity, relationship or family (marriage or dating status, number of children, functioning level of family), popularity, school grades, mistakes, moods, job or athletic performance, skill levels, and control over events. It can be difficult to separate core worth from externals when the media suggests that one is less than worthwhile if one isn't powerful, wealthy, young, and beautiful. However, as the dying wise man counseled his young friend before his death in *Tuesdays with Morrie* (Albom 1997, 42), "The culture we have does not make people feel good about ourselves. And you have to be strong enough to say if the culture doesn't work, don't buy it." Once we are sure of our equal intrinsic worth, then we are relieved of the need to compete in order to establish worth. We are less inclined to judge ourselves and compare ourselves to others. In short, we become more secure in our own worth, and thus in ourselves.

Sometimes very bright people have difficulty separating inner worth from externals. They ask how someone can have worth when they are not valued by others or when they feel so worthless. Consider a child who has not accomplished much of anything yet. Why is that child so precious to his or her parents? Partly because the parents have chosen to value the child. Partly because each child has innate qualities that we enjoy (the delight of the child at play, for example). Despite the child's inexperience and rough edges, he or she also has unlimited potential to love, beautify, comfort, laugh, change course when mistakes are made, be patient, be gentle, be persistent, develop, and make the world a better place in countless other ways. We adults can also choose to value our own innate worth and capacities. And as we look back over our lives and remember the ways we have contributed to the well-being of ourselves and others, in any way large or small, we are reminded that no one is worthless.

BUILDING BLOCK 2: UNCONDITIONAL LOVE

The psychologist Abraham Maslow (Lowry 1973) noted that psychological health is not possible without love for the essential core. Children with self-esteem tend to have parents who love them. These parents show interest in the children's lives, treat them with respect, encourage and support them as they strive to attain high standards, and care about them enough to set reasonable limits. The good news is that even those who did not experience this type of parental love can learn to become good parents to themselves.

What is love? I suggest that love is (1) a feeling that we experience, (2) the attitude that wants what is best for the beloved at each and every moment, (3) a decision and commitment made each day (even if we don't feel like it), and (4) a skill that we learn. If the core is like a seed, then love is the nourishment that helps the seed grow. Love does not create worth (it already exists). However, love helps us experience our worth and enjoy the process of growing. Even though we might not always have the love of others, we can always choose to love ourselves.

Each individual person has been created to love and be loved.

—Mother Teresa

BUILDING BLOCK 3: GROWTH

We tend to feel better about ourselves when we are living constructively—making reasonable decisions, developing desirable attributes, and polishing the rough edges around the core.

Thus, we might think of building block 3 as the process of completing, coming to flower, or putting love into action. Growing is a direction and a process, not reaching a destination. Growing does not change our core worth, but it helps us to experience it with greater satisfaction. The inner core can grow even as the body ages or becomes infirm. As the concentration camp survivor Viktor Frankl (1959) noted, people can attain inner freedom even though their bodies are imprisoned. We grow as we try to lift others along with ourselves, as we develop in character and personality, and as we discover ways to enjoy wholesome pleasures.

Exercise: Start with the End in Mind

Consider some of the main points that we have explored so far: Self-esteem is a quiet and relatively unshakeable sense of satisfaction that comes from recognizing and appreciating our existing worth, and then choosing to love and grow. Self-esteem is not comparative and competitive. That is, we do not acquire worth by outshining others. Instead, we learn to recognize and experience our worth. Self-esteem does not boast or put others down. Rather, one with self-esteem considers the well-being of others as well as the well-being of oneself. Self-esteem can be built through persistent effort. The building process is one that involves seeing clearly, loving, and developing.

For a few moments, reflect upon the following:

How might you appreciate yourself when you are imperfect, are mistreated, or compare less favorably to others?

What would be the positive consequences of appreciating yourself more?

2 | Be Mindful

Our experiences in life and our perception of externals can change the way we feel about ourselves. The wonderful news, however, is that we can learn how to develop self-esteem. In building self-esteem, effective attempts will target thoughts, images, feelings, and behaviors. Which do you think makes the best starting point? Imagine a cycle that looks like this:

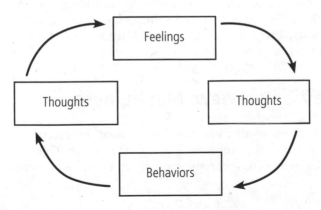

Figure 3

A parent gives a child an age-appropriate task, such as taking out the trash (behavior). When the child succeeds, he or she is praised and thinks, "I can do it; the world is reasonable" (thoughts). The child then feels confident, which leads to more constructive thoughts such as "I can probably do other things and succeed." As a result, the child might pick up an instrument and learn to play it (behavior). This in turn leads to more constructive thoughts, which lead to more feelings of confidence, and the cycle continues in a way that strengthens self-esteem. Got the picture? I will often show this cycle to adults and ask, "So where do you think is the best place to intervene when trying to build self-esteem—thoughts, behavior, or feelings?" People usually respond that it is best to jump in at the behaviors and thoughts level. Nothing wrong with that—in a cyclical model there is no wrong answer. However, consider this: Where do parents of a newborn intervene when they hold the baby to the breast, embrace him or her, or look into the baby's eyes and smile? Are they teaching the baby how to think and behave? (Are they saying, "I love you because you are so smart and will become the CEO of a large corporation?") Or are they affecting the baby's feelings? It's an interesting question. Usually we adults choose to start with thoughts and behaviors. It seems safer and more concrete, and our thoughts and behaviors are important. But the attitudes of the heart, I wish to suggest, are at least as important.

The Tibetan View: Mindfulness

Mindfulness meditation has been found in recent years to improve a wide range of medical and psychological conditions, ranging from chronic pain to stress, anxiety, depression, sleep disorders, and eating disorders. It appears to increase activity in the area of the brain associated with happiness and optimism. Practitioners of mindfulness often feel more self-confident and comfortable in their own skin despite external events. In fact, results have been so impressive that mindfulness meditation is now being taught in academic medical centers, pain clinics, hospitals, and schools (including law schools) all over the world.

Mindfulness meditation was introduced to Western medical circles in 1979 by Jon Kabat-Zinn, Ph.D., at the University of Massachusetts Medical School, and is based on the Theravada Buddhist tradition. This tradition explores the working of the mind and considers how people can be happier and suffer less. Mindfulness is respectful of and compatible with other traditions because it does not judge one approach as better or worse. In the foreword to Kabat-Zinn's book *Full Catastrophe Living*, Joan Borysenko, Ph.D., noted that "mindfulness is more than a meditation practice that can have profound medical and psychological benefits; it is also a way of life that reveals the gentle and loving wholeness that lies at the heart of our being, even in times of great pain and suffering" (1990, xvii). Perhaps you already notice that the mindfulness approach is consistent with the concepts we explored in chapter 1.

The peaceful Tibetan masters teach that we are of two minds: the wisdom mind and the ordinary mind (Rinpoche 1993). (Refer to figure 4 on the next page.)

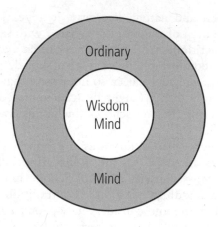

Figure 4

WISDOM MIND AND ORDINARY MIND

The wisdom mind represents our true happy nature, which is similar to the core self. The wisdom mind, like the core depicted in chapter 1, is kind, wise, and compassionate—it desires the happiness of others as much as that of ourselves (which is why it is happy), and it is good humored, hopeful, peaceful, simple, and integrated. The wisdom mind is characterized by self-esteem and dignity, but also humility—realizing that all people possess the wisdom mind. However, the ordinary mind surrounds the wisdom mind like a dark cloud, keeping us unaware of our true happy nature and causing much suffering (Rinpoche 1993).

The ordinary mind attaches to swirling, racing thoughts and disturbing negative emotions. When we say "I am beside myself with anger (or worry)," we mean that we are caught up in the ordinary mind and separated from our wisdom mind. Mindfulness meditation teaches methods of getting beneath these scattered thoughts and distressing feelings to rest in the peaceful wholeness of the wisdom mind.

Young children do not appear to experience self-dislike. As we age, however, we learn to endlessly think, judge, compare, criticize, worry, blame, obsess about faults, evaluate, and fight against the way life is. We demand that life, or our selves, be different, and we get angry when we don't get what we think we must have. We fear losing what we do have, and we feel sad when we lose what we think we need in order to be happy. Mindfulness teaches people how to release the ordinary mind's attachments that keep us unhappy, and how to rest in the wisdom mind. When agitated water is allowed to settle, it becomes very clear. Likewise, when we allow our minds to settle, we can see clearly once again. (Later in the book, we'll explore meditation methods that help us to do this.)

In mindfulness meditation, the attitudes of the heart are very important. In fact, in many of the Asian languages, the word for "mind" is the same as the word for "heart." Fairly early in the teaching of this approach, Jon Kabat-Zinn (1990) introduces the attitudes of mindfulness. However, we might think of these as attitudes of "heartfulness," reminding ourselves that these attitudes are deeper than the chatter of the mind and are experienced in the body. Let's explore these, as they embody the emotional goals of self-esteem building and form the emotional foundation for our journey.

Heartfulness Attitudes

The ten attitudes of heartfulness, adapted from a work by Jon Kabat-Zinn (1990), suggest a different way of being—a new way of relating to ourselves and the world.

1. **Patience.** Growth takes a long time. When we plant a tomato seed, we do not stomp it

and loudly criticize it for not being a tomato. Instead we gently place it in fertile soil and make sure it gets plenty of water and sunlight. And when a sprout emerges from the soil, we say, "Oh boy, it's growing." We continue to nurture the plant at all times and take satisfaction in the process. To be patient is to trust and never give up on the growth process, without making angry demands and expectations or worrying that the seed won't flourish properly. We usually can't foresee just how and when our efforts will bear fruit. "Patience is a bitter plant, but it has sweet fruit," as a German proverb goes. Or, as another saying goes, "One must wait until evening to see how splendid the day has been."

2. **Acceptance.** Acceptance means to take in, or welcome. To accept, then, is to see clearly and with full awareness the good and bad, suffering and joy, as part of life, and to experience life without battling, insisting that things be different, or immediately trying to change, fix, or get rid of the present distress. Even if we are unsure of what to do, we can dispassionately observe, "This is the way things are right now." Once we can accurately see the situation, then we are free to decide what to do—whether to act constructively or allow the situation to be as it is without resisting it.

When we accept guests in our home, we receive them with pleasure just as they are. When we accept ourselves, we experience ourselves with a similar welcoming attitude. We are aware of our weaknesses (and perhaps become determined to improve so that we might experience ourselves with even greater pleasure). We also recognize that we are not perfect and cannot will ourselves to immediately become perfect. So we accept ourselves as we are, for now. We would do this for a child, and we can learn to do this with ourselves. As the psychologist Carl Rogers observed, "The curious paradox is that when I accept myself just as I am, then I can change" (1987, 17).

Broader than self-acceptance, acceptance means that we also welcome the world as it is. That is, we take in all situations and the range of resulting feelings—embarrassment, fear, shame, rejection, sadness, disappointment, and so on—and allow them to be just as they are. In letting go of aversion to negative feelings, we become unafraid to completely feel those feelings. We turn toward them, rather than away. Knowing that feelings come and go, we calmly and patiently watch them arise and subside at their own pace, saying to ourselves, "Whatever I am feeling is okay; it is okay to just feel it."

Acceptance does not mean passivity, resignation, or complacency. It simply means seeing things as they are. And when the decision to act becomes clear, then we can also act with acceptance, and without impulsivity, resistance, or the like. The paradox is that when we release our death grip on control, we gain a greater sense of inner control ("Even if the situation doesn't improve, I'll be okay"). We gain more confidence in our ability to manage strong emotions.

When we experience pain or discomfort, the natural inclination is to try to avoid the pain or do something to get rid of the source of the pain. In the case of outer discomfort caused by a neighbor's loud radio, for example, we might take a drive to get away from the noise or ask the neighbor to turn down the volume. However, for inner pain this kind of approach is usually counterproductive. For example, one who fears a panic attack tenses up and tries to fight it. This makes the panic attack more intense and longer lasting. A better approach would be to relax, and let the attack come and then pass. Similarly, people who have experienced traumatic events may try fruitlessly to get rid of the memories. It would be better to accept and process the memory. If someone experiences chronic pain, one of the worst things to do is to tense up and fight it. Often learning to just notice the pain, watching it come and go, helps to diminish the pain. Tensing, wincing, bracing, or wishing things weren't as they are will increase the fight-or-flight response, which exacerbates distress. Trying to avoid the pain by running away, sedating oneself with drugs, shopping, watching TV, or using some other form of avoidance only causes the distress to return with greater intensity. Similarly, noticing our faults and negative feelings, and holding them in full, compassionate awareness changes the way we relate to distress.

3. **Compassion.** Perhaps the central and most important attitude, compassion is sorrow over the suffering of others, and a desire to help. It is closely aligned with love, or

loving-kindness, which is the type of universal or undifferentiated love that considers the worth and needs of all humans. The Dalai Lama has noted that in the West compassion is an attitude that is only extended toward others. In Tibet, compassion is felt toward others *and* self. He adds that in Tibet he does not see low self-esteem or depression, because people there experience compassion toward all people (Goleman 2003).

The following story of compassion (Hinckley 2000, 28–29) tells of two boys who were walking along a road that led through a field. "They saw an old coat and a badly worn pair of men's shoes by the roadside, and, in the distance, they saw the owner working in the field. The younger boy suggested that they hide the shoes, conceal themselves, and watch the perplexity on the owner's face when he returned. The older boy, a benevolent lad, thought that would not be so good. He said the owner must be a very poor man. After discussing the matter, they concluded to try another experiment. Instead of hiding the shoes, they would put a silver dollar in each one and, concealing themselves, see what the owner did when he discovered the money.

"Soon the man returned from the field, put on his coat, slipped one foot into a shoe, felt something hard, took it out, and found a silver dollar. Wonder and surprise showed in his face. He looked at the dollar again and again, turned around and could see nobody, then proceeded to put on the other shoe where, to his great surprise, he found another dollar. His feelings overcame him and he knelt down and offered aloud a prayer of thanksgiving, in which he spoke of his wife being sick and helpless and his children without bread." After invoking a blessing on his benefactors, the man left, and the boys walked down the road, glad for the good feeling that their compassion had wrought.

Frank Robinson, a highly talented player who was honored by the National Baseball Hall of Fame and became a respected Major League baseball coach, recently had to pull his third-string catcher out of a game in the middle of an inning. The catcher had made two errors and had been unable to prevent seven stolen bases. Robinson's team won the game, and the catcher, with gracious acceptance, said, "If my daddy was managing the team, I'm sure he would have done the same thing." However, as tears streamed down Robinson's face at the post-game press conference, he said, "I feel for him ... I just appreciate him hanging in there as long as he did ... It was not his fault. We know his shortcoming[s]. They took advantage of them today. I felt like I had to do [it] for the good of the club." Robinson's reaction was a remarkable display of compassion.

Mother Teresa said that each individual person has been created to love and be loved. Love heals wounds and nurtures growth. We admire people who demonstrate compassion and know how good it feels to experience it, both as the giver and receiver. So in our effort to develop heartfulness we form the intention to be compassionate toward all people, including our self—to experience loving-kindness as we struggle, to have the intention to help as we try to overcome suffering.

4. **Nonjudgment.** A young child plays without inhibition. Later, the child learns to evaluate and judge. Do you ever stop to consider how often we adults do this? We say, "I'm not good at this," "I'm stupid," "I'm not as good as Mary," "Why can't I be better than I am?" "Why is my self-esteem so low?" "I stink," "I should be improving faster," "I'm not doing as well as I did yesterday," "I don't like the way I am," "I'll never get better," "What if I don't get promoted?" "It's awful to be feeling afraid," or "I shouldn't be feeling sad." But which works better, a carrot or a stick? Does saying mean things motivate effectively? Or do loving-kindness and encouragement work better? A person who puts him- or herself down finds it more difficult to rise. As a tennis coach said, "Sometimes you just have to stop the negative thinking and judgments that get in the way. Just think, 'Bounce, hit.'" Watch what happens, without judging yourself. It can be quite liberating to realize that we don't have to overreact to situations by issuing harsh, punishing judgments that lead to intense negative emotions. We just note what is happening and respond as well as we can. If you *do* notice that you are judging yourself or your performance, don't judge the judging. Thank the ordinary mind for trying to help you improve, and then calmly bring your mind back to what you are doing in the present moment.

5. **Nonattachment.** The Eastern masters teach that attachment is the root of unhappiness. Thus, if I insist that I need a certain kind of car in order to be happy, I might be sad if I don't have it. If I get that car, I might fear that it will be damaged. Or I might become angry if it gets scratched or stolen. Similarly, if I am attached to my body, my self-esteem might be lowered as I age or put on a few pounds. So we can practice loosening our grip on what we demand in order to have happiness and self-esteem, trusting that we already have everything we need for those two things. This is not meant to suggest that appreciating and taking care of one's body is unimportant—only that externals (money, recognition, appearance, roles, and the like) are not the source of self-esteem or happiness.

In India and Africa, monkeys are caught by attaching a treat-filled coconut to a string. The coconut has a hole large enough for the monkey to insert his open hand. Once the monkey clamps his fist on the banana or sweet meats inside the coconut, the fist becomes too large to withdraw. Unwilling to release the grip, the monkey can be easily captured. In Tonga, the octopus is a delicacy. Fishermen dangle a simple lure made from a stone and shells called a *maka-feke* from their canoes. The octopus clamps on to the lure and is then pulled into the boat (Monson 2006). In both cases, the attachment is the problem. Various forms of meditation teach us to release—to loosen our grip on the things that can prevent us from experiencing happiness—and relax into our wisdom minds, where the capacity for happiness already exists. Paradoxically, as we release externals and stop struggling so hard to be something we are not, we gain a greater appreciation of who we are.

6.   **Beginner's mind.** The expert's mind is closed to new learning and experience. The beginner's mind is open to these. Throughout this book you will be asked to approach the principles and skills offered herein with an open mind, the mind of a child who is experiencing something for the first time, without overlying expectations or assumptions. Don't automatically assume that the way you experience yourself cannot change. Try to balance a healthy skepticism with a playful openness to try something new.

7.   **Good humor.** Much of psychopathology is the tendency to be overly serious about our present condition, to take life too seriously. We have to laugh at ourselves because we all do ridiculous things at times. One of life's greatest challenges is how to enjoy it. As you try the skills in this book, please try to maintain a spark of good humor and of playfulness.

8.   **Commitment.** In a loving relationship one commits to the growth of that relationship. We form an intention ("May we be happy," for example) and look for ways to encourage growth. In building self-esteem, we create a similar intention. Committing also means that we will practice the necessary skills even when we don't feel like it. As mountaineer William H. Murray said, "the moment one definitely

commits oneself, then Providence moves too"
(1951, 7).

9. **Vastness.** The wisdom mind is expansive, deep,
and wide enough to contain any thoughts and
feelings with equanimity. When we are resting
in the wisdom mind, it is as if we are deep in
the peaceful, quiet depths of the ocean. From
this vantage point, we can dispassionately and
compassionately watch unpleasant thoughts
and feelings as though they were waves rising
on the surface and then being absorbed into
the vast ocean. This attitude helps us to be
calmly aware, without being drawn into
harmful judgments about ourselves or the situations we encounter.

10. **Generosity.** Despite being one of the most
important attitudes, generosity is no longer
emphasized very much in Western cultures,
which increasingly seem to favor the acquisi-
tion and hoarding of material wealth. The generous heart gives from a sense of worth, not a
need to prove one's worth, knowing that one's
giving matters. Giving can be very simple—a
smile, our full attention, patience, allowing
people to be just as they are (the gift of acceptance), courtesy, a helping hand, encouragement, food, or money—offering what we can,
insofar as this does not create undue hardship
for ourselves. What does this have to do with
self-esteem? Generosity generates a number of
intangible benefits. We see joy in the recipients'
faces that makes us feel glad and connected to
others. Giving helps us to let go of attachments
as we realize after we give things away that we

are really whole, already possessing within us the seeds of happiness. We might think of generosity as practice opening up the grasping fist and letting go of things that are illusory or not needed for our happiness.

Giving is empowering in other ways as well. Sometimes we avoid people who are struggling, fearing that their suffering might contaminate us and drag us down. In so doing we close ourselves off from the joy of giving and loving. When we give with a soft, open, nonjudgmental heart, we see that we all are connected. We all suffer for similar reasons, but we are vast enough to contain suffering with equanimity and kindness.

Exercise: Applying the Heartfulness Attitudes

In a separate notebook, describe a self-esteem issue difficulty that you are having. Then describe how you might approach this issue using all or a few of the ten heartfulness attitudes. You might find it helpful to recall times in your life when you experienced or witnessed these attitudes. For example, can you think of a time when you were patient with yourself? When others were patient with you or themselves?

3 Clear Away Negative Thoughts

S elf-esteem enables us to experience ourselves accurately and gladly. What prevents us from doing so? Unreasonably negative thoughts—which surround and camouflage the core like a cloud of debris after a storm. Cognitive therapy (CT) is the branch of psychology that helps people identify, challenge, and then replace such thoughts. This well-researched approach is considered a mainstream treatment for depression, anxiety, and problem anger. Because self-esteem is so strongly related to these conditions, CT is also very useful for self-esteem building.

Aaron Beck, MD (1976), and Albert Ellis, Ph.D. (Ellis and Harper 1975), developed similar approaches for helping people reshape their thinking habits. Their approaches depict the way thoughts influence our emotions as follows:

Adversity   ⟶   *Thoughts*   ⟶   *Emotions*

Adversity represents a distressing event or situation. For instance, let's say that Paula and Lisa grew up with an extremely abusive father. In response to the abuse (adversity), Paula thinks, "I've been treated so poorly. I must not be worth anything." As a result she feels depressed and experiences herself with dislike (emotions). Lisa responds to the same kind of abuse with different thoughts. She tells herself, "He might treat me like dirt, but that's *not* who I am inside." Lisa is upset by the abusive treatment, but she preserves her self-esteem and optimism. What determines whether we experience appropriate upset or disturbance at the emotional level is the thoughts that we choose.

CT shows that the thoughts affecting our emotions pass through our minds so quickly that we hardly notice them, let alone stop to test them for reasonableness. Dr. Beck calls these *automatic thoughts* (ATs). ATs that are unreasonably negative— judgmental, unkind, and inaccurate thoughts that make us feel dissatisfied and uncomfortable with ourselves—are called *distortions*.

CT assumes that people are very capable of reasonable thinking. However, because we are imperfect, we might draw faulty conclusions from the faulty data we receive. Consider, for example, what children think about where babies come from before they have all the facts. They might assume that the stork brings them, that hospitals dispense them, or that they grow in the mother's stomach. Their thinking becomes more reasonable when they acquire the facts. In the example above, Paula bought her father's message that she was worthless— not because it was true, but because she did not challenge the message. CT asserts that people can quickly and efficiently learn to identify their thought patterns, challenge them, and then replace distortions with more reasonable thoughts. As they do so, they gain a measure of control over both their thoughts and their emotions.

Our thinking patterns, for bad or good, are influenced by a number of factors. For example, the events we experience can influence our thoughts. Thus, someone who is abused sexually or physically might think, "I was treated as an object, so I must be one." One's social environment, which might include the media, one's friends, and one's family, can also influence the way we learn to think. For example, a father might embrace his daughter upon learning that she has been raped and simply say, "That must have been so hard." How different the daughter's thoughts would be if he instead judged her or questioned her motives. Similarly, the emotions and self-esteem of soldiers can be influenced by the support they experience upon returning from a war. Our physical condition—our state of health, or how rested, nourished, and conditioned we are—also affects our ability to think clearly. Finally, our coping skills and behavioral patterns can influence our thinking. Other chapters in this book will address these factors that influence our thoughts.

Although events can influence our thinking, a basic assumption of CT is that we are ultimately responsible for the thoughts that we choose. We can't always control the way others treat us. However, we are completely free to control our thoughts. This assumption does not blame people for lacking self-esteem. Rather, it empowers us to realize that we can shape the thoughts that influence self-esteem and avoid blaming others for our present feelings.

Distorted Thinking

So, let's explore the basic types of distortions (Beck 1995; Ellis and Harper 1975) and how they can be modified. Because there are only a handful of distortions, you can learn them and their replacement thoughts so you can prevent yourself from falling into the common thinking traps. With practice you will learn to replace distortions quickly and without much effort, because this is what stressful situations often require.

ALL-OR-NOTHING THINKING

Here you hold yourself up to a perfect, or near-perfect, standard. If you fail to "clear the bar" you conclude that you are worthless. There is no middle ground or partial credit for effort. For example, a bright and likeable student once told me that he was very troubled over a creative writing assignment. The prospect of getting anything less than an A had him feeling depressed and suicidal. Eventually, he discovered the distortion: "In my culture, if you don't reach your goals, you don't deserve to live," he told me. I asked him, "Where is it written that someone who isn't perfect is worthless?" He thought for a while and said, "That's the first time someone has told me that I don't have to be perfect in order to be worthwhile." Others might question their worth should they fail to earn a certain salary, lose an argument, or make a mistake. If you must judge, try judging performance only, not the core self. You might think, "I batted about eight hundred on this task. That's pretty good. Next time I'll try to do things a bit differently."

LABELING

Have you ever noticed that people often label themselves harshly? "I'm dumb." "I'm such a loser." "I'm boring." "What an idiot! Why am I so stupid?" (Notice that this last utterance really isn't a question as much as it is an expression of resentment. People who use such expressions are more likely to be depressed because they keep themselves feeling stuck and powerless.) You might ask if such unkind judgments really serve to motivate as well as encouragement does. On the other hand, you might think, "A loser never wins, so why try?" Here's why a negative label is unreasonable. When you say "I am stupid (or dumb, or boring)," you are saying that you are stupid *always* and in *every* situation. This is clearly not true. Howard Gardner (1993) of Harvard, for example, notes that there are different ways to manifest intelligence. Some might show their intelligence through either mathematic or verbal skills. Others might demonstrate intelligence through personal (emotional intelligence) skills, interpersonal (people) skills, music, art (or other spatial skills), or body skills (such as athletics or dance). The antidote to negative labeling? Again, if you must judge, judge only the behavior (saying "I didn't do too well today on this," for example). The core is too complex to be described by a simple label.

OVERGENERALIZING

Ask a pessimist or someone with low self-esteem to explain why he got into an argument with his spouse and he is likely to say something like "I'm not very swift" (giving himself a label). He is likely to make it worse by also thinking "I *always* mess up relationships. I *never* get them right." However, it is less judgmental and more precise to think "I (or, perhaps, we) haven't learned how to handle this difficult topic calmly." In addition to using "always" and "never," one who overgeneralizes also tends to use words like "nobody" and "everybody." Rodney Dangerfield quipped that his psychiatrist once told him, "Don't be ridiculous. Everybody doesn't hate you. Everybody doesn't know you." An antidote to overgeneralization is to use the word "some." It's usually more accurate to think "Sometimes I do fairly well. Some people like me, at least somewhat."

ASSUMING

"Yes," you might think, "but I *know* that that waiter dislikes me. Look at the way he treated me." This could be the distortion known as mind reading. That waiter may or may not dislike you. He might simply be angry about something that happened to him twenty minutes or twenty years before. He might be quite annoyed at something you did, but he may not dislike you. So his dislike of you is just one possibility. You won't know if he actually does feel that way unless you check it out. In another example, let's say you've been invited to your neighborhood block party. You might assume that if you go to the block party everyone will in fact dislike you and you'll have a miserable time. This could be the distortion known as fortune-telling or predicting the future. In fact, some might like you, some might dislike you, and some might hardly notice you. You could go to the party with an open or beginner's mind and just observe what happens. Sometimes good things happen, too.

EMOTIONAL REASONING

Can you remember a teacher who "made you" feel dumb? Now when you confront a new and challenging situation do you still feel inadequate and thus think that you really are inadequate? Or perhaps you once made an unwise decision and felt so ashamed that you concluded that you are worthless. Automatically equating feelings with reality is called *emotional reasoning*. We can be open to and accepting of feelings, but we can also recognize that feelings don't necessarily represent reality. Remind yourself that negative feelings are signals of upset, not statements of fact. Challenge the underlying thoughts. Asking "What would 100 percent inadequate, worthless, or bad be like?" helps you to avoid all-or-nothing thinking.

DWELLING ON THE NEGATIVE

Suppose that you have a beautiful garden. One plant is not doing so well, so you focus exclusively on that struggling plant. Soon you forget to notice the other beautiful plants. Likewise, you might dwell on a mistake or shortcoming to the point that you ruin your self-esteem, or even your life. You fail to take into account all the good that exists, all the good that you have done. When you look into the mirror, do you zero in on what's wrong? Or do you notice what's right—your overall appearance, your smile, and so on? When you find yourself dwelling on what's wrong in yourself or your life, you might think, "Okay, perhaps this is something I can work on. In the meantime, what else is going on? What can I notice that is going well? What would a friend notice in addition to the faults?" A man once joked to his neighbor, "Why are you so happy? Your life is just as bad as mine." Perhaps the happy person is taking the time to see the bigger picture and appreciate what *isn't* wrong.

REJECTING THE POSITIVE

Whereas dwelling on the negative overlooks positives, this distortion actually negates positives. Imagine that someone compliments you for doing a good job. You say, "No big deal." However, it would be much more satisfying to thank the person and think, "I'm really glad that I was able to figure out what was required and do a good job." Then you'd be validating both the giver of the compliment and yourself.

MAKING UNFAVORABLE COMPARISONS

How satisfying it can be to exert ourselves, invest our talents, and attain goals related to hobbies, education, profession, recreation, meaningful causes, or relationships. The examples set by those we respect and admire can inspire us and suggest possibilities. Trouble arises, however, when we begin to compare ourselves to others. Now inspiration turns to judgment: "I'm not as smart as Wayne." "Sandra is a better golfer than I am." "John is much more popular than I am." "I wish I could be as successful as Randi—she's a bright manager and I'm just a salesman." In each case we get the short end of the stick, and self-esteem suffers.

The antidote to this distortion is to simply stop comparing and recognize that each person contributes in unique ways at his or her own unique pace. I'll ask my students, "Who is more important, a surgeon or a general practitioner?" They might answer, "Well, a surgeon might resolve an acute crisis, but the general practitioner might prevent it from occurring." "Who is more worthwhile, a surgeon or a physical therapist?" I ask. "Well, the surgeon can save a life, but the therapist might help to restore physical function and hope," they respond. When we consider who is more important to the nation's health, the doctor or the garbage collector, we soon realize that people contribute in very different ways. Why must we compare and judge? As we step back to see the bigger picture, we begin to see that each person has a different blend of strengths and weaknesses. Also, as we compare ourselves to shining examples of success, we can remember that each person, even an expert, struggles in certain areas.

SHOULDS, OUGHTS, AND MUSTS

"Should" statements are perfectionistic, rigid demands that we make of ourselves, perhaps hoping that such demands will help us to overcome the discomfort of being imperfect. Examples include the following: "I should not make mistakes," "I should have known better," "I ought to be better," "I must not fail," and "I must be a perfect boss [or spouse, or child]." There is a punitive, scolding quality to these demands. Although we'd hope that these demands would motivate us to do better, they usually just make us feel worse. For example, how do you feel when you tell yourself that you must perform perfectly, and then you don't? In fact, research suggests that we tend to perform better when we strive to do a good job, not a perfect job, because we are not as uptight when we are just trying to do a good job.

What would it mean if you didn't perfectly achieve what you feel that you must or should? Would it mean that you are worthless, or just imperfect? Perhaps the only reasonable "should" tells us that we should be just as we are, given our imperfect background, experience, skill levels, and understanding. Some would say that a kinder and more effective way to motivate people is to replace the demands with "would," "could," "want," "choose," and "prefer" statements. So instead of saying "I should," "I ought to," or "I must," we might think "I want to improve" "I choose to work hard," "I would very much like to win the competition," "I want to be a loving parent," "It would be great to reach that goal," or "I wonder how I could improve; what would it take?" Please be aware, though, that "should" statements can be very difficult to release. It often helps to realize that giving up the "should" does not mean giving up a cherished value, such as working hard or doing one's best. It simply frees us to approach the goal in a more enjoyable, less judgmental, and, we hope, more effective way.

CATASTROPHIZING

When we catastrophize, we take something that is uncomfortable (such as embarrassment or fear of failure) and determine that it is unbearable, devastating, intolerable, and terrible. We might think, for example, "I would never give a speech. I might stumble and people would laugh. That would be awful!" or "It would be horrible if I were rejected," or "I can't stand it when my boss criticizes me." Such statements increase fear and arousal and undermine confidence. We might tense up and thus perform below our abilities. We might even begin to avoid challenging situations, thus depriving ourselves of opportunities to master our fears and enhance self-esteem. Catastrophizing often begins with a fearful possibility (such as "I might fail"), which leads to a negative conclusion ("I'll probably fail; I'll make people angry and disappointed"), and results in an expectation of the worst ("This will be awful. Nothing could be worse"). In reality, when we stop catastrophizing, we become calmer and think more clearly. We learn that we can indeed bear adversity, although it is not necessarily convenient or comfortable. Catastrophizing is challenged by thinking "Okay, I don't like this, but I can indeed bear it," "It could be worse. Nobody is shooting at me. It will pass," or "I really can get through this." With these replacement thoughts, we learn to turn toward what we fear, rather than away from it, with calm and full acceptance. In so doing, we become more self-confident.

PERSONALIZING

Personalizing is thinking that you are more responsible or involved than the facts indicate. For example, a rape victim typically thinks that the crime is her fault, rather than the fault of the perpetrator. Or a man might question what he did to deserve his spouse's angry outbursts, not realizing that his wife was mad at the world that day.

Personalizing is an attempt to have more control than we actually have. Ironically, the attempt backfires, since reality reminds us that we have less control than we want. We don't make people do what they do and we can't always prevent people from feeling pain. The solution to personalizing is to ask, "Why might someone behave that way? Is it possible that this really isn't about me?"

BLAMING

Whereas personalizing places too much responsibility on ourselves, blaming places too much responsibility on others. For example, we might say, "I blame my drinking problems on my parents; they made me drink," or "I have low self-esteem because my spouse left me." The more we avoid taking responsibility for our own well-being, the more we feel helpless and out of control. So we might instead think, "Yes, this was a difficult situation. Now I take responsibility for moving past it."

Exercise: Distortions Review

Now, let's look at how the bread and butter of CT, the daily thought record, is used. This record is most effective when you already have a reasonable mastery of the distortions. Before you get started, review the list of distortions above, and then quiz yourself by thinking of an everyday example of each type of distortion and coming up with a replacement thought for each.

Applying Cognitive Therapy: The Daily Thought Record

A tenet of CT is that we don't improve without practice. The daily thought record is the basic tool that helps us to slow down our thinking in order to catch and replace the distortions that we habitually use.

Identify a situation that undermines your self-esteem, and the feelings that result. Rate each of the feelings from 1 to 10, with 1 meaning no disturbance and 10 meaning severe disturbance. Then make a numbered list of your automatic thoughts (ATs) in that situation, and go back and write down the distortions in parentheses. Next, for each AT write down a replacement thought that is more rational. Finally, rate the related feelings again and notice any shift in intensity. Any reduction in intensity is worthwhile. Below is an example of a daily thought record.

Distressing Situation (Adversity):
I failed my promotion test.

Resulting Feeling(s)	Before Writing Replacement Thoughts	After Writing Replacement Thoughts
Depressed	9	5
Anxious	7	5

Automatic Thoughts (Distortions)	Replacement Thoughts
1. I'm an idiot. (labeling)	1. This was a tough test. I'll prepare better next time.
2. I screw up everything. (overgeneralizing)	2. This is one test. I do a number of things well or I wouldn't have been recommended for promotion.
3. Everyone did better than I did. (overgeneralizing)	3. Some did better, but some did worse than I did.
4. Joe aced it. He's so much smarter than I am. (making unfavorable comparisons)	4. Joe is an excellent test taker. I have other strengths. We're just different.
5. I'll fail the retest. It will be awful. (assuming and catastrophizing)	5. If I prepare more effectively I might pass. I hope I do. If I don't pass, I can indeed live with it, although I'd prefer to have the additional pay.

DEFUSING

In his brilliant book about acceptance and commitment therapy (ACT, pronounced "act"), *Get Out of Your Mind and Into Your Life*, Steven C. Hayes, Ph.D. (2005), asserts that almost all people suffer some form of intense inner pain at some times in their lives. The suffering might be depression, anxiety, substance abuse, or self-dislike and suicidal thoughts, and it results from the battles we wage against our thoughts as we futilely try to get rid of our histories.

Let's go back to our example of the teacher (or other person) who made you feel dumb. Years later, the suffering could be avoided by simply staying away from that teacher (and perhaps the subject, such as math). However, the problem-solving mind doesn't let it end there. It goes on the attack, thinking "What if I really am dumb? I hate feeling dumb. I can't be dumb. If I try hard enough I won't be dumb. I've got to stop thinking that I'm dumb. If I really try I won't think I'm dumb anymore." It's as if a war is raging in the mind, a war that doesn't end as we get locked into the struggle with the past.

Hayes calls this process *fusion*. We struggle so long against negative thoughts, which we assume are true, that we eventually become identified with the thoughts. The problem-solving mind usually works well in getting rid of outside problems, like a leaky faucet. However, the more we try to get rid of inner problems (for example, by thinking about the past), the more fused we become with the past. We can't get rid of the past event. And, the more we try not to think about it, the more we think about it, experience the suffering, and even become the suffering.

You can test this idea. First, really think about a white elephant for a few moments. Now block out the image and try not to think about the white elephant at all. Count how many times you actually think of the white elephant. Of course, you will think often of the white elephant despite your efforts to get rid of the idea.

Similarly, we might try to escape pain through avoidance (using substances, shopping, watching television, working, and so on). This only works temporarily, and then the pain returns more strongly. The more we try to numb the pain by shutting off our emotions, the more we lose our capacities for joy and engagement with life. So a different approach, defusion, can be helpful.

The goal of defusing is to confront our distressing histories without attachment or aversion, but with complete acceptance, compassion, and equanimity. *Complete* acceptance doesn't mean saying, "Okay, I'll do this exercise quickly so that I can get rid of my pain." It means choosing to completely and fully let the pain in with a kind, welcoming, dispassionate attitude. Then we can commit to living our lives fully, carrying whatever pain that remains with full acceptance. We still have the thoughts, but we kindly watch them from a distance without buying into them. It's as if the war continues to rage, but we've stepped away from the battlefield, and we watch the war from a distance with detachment. Hayes (2005) suggests the following defusing strategies.

Exercise: Identify the Source of the Pain

I. List a few painful situations from the past that might have hurt your self-esteem in some way. Maybe you were embarrassed, rejected, shamed, disrespected, abused, or ridiculed. Perhaps you made a bad decision or lost your composure. In addition to having painful thoughts about these situations, you probably also experience painful feelings, memories, images, and/or bodily sensations when you think about them. Simply notice these reactions.

2. Next, write down how long each situation has bothered you.

3. Finally, rather than trying to get rid of these problems, just let them into your awareness with a soft and open attitude. You might think, "These are just memories."

Exercise: Milk, Milk, Milk

1. For a few moments fully experience milk in your mind—how it looks, feels, and tastes. You might experience it as cold, white, and creamy.

2. Now say the word "milk" out loud and repeat it as many times as you can in forty-five seconds. Then notice what happens. People often notice that the experience changes. The meaning falls away from the word, and the word just becomes a sound.

3. Now take a negative thought about yourself that you associate with one of the painful situations that you listed above. Perhaps the thought is self-critical and harsh. Put the thought into a single word, such as "bad," "loser," "dumb," or "immature."

4. Rate from 1 to 10 how distressing the word is. Then rate how believable it is.

5. Welcome the word and other aspects of the memory into your awareness with complete, kind acceptance.

6. Repeat the word out loud as many times as you can for a period of forty-five seconds.

Now, again rate how distressing the word is. Did the level of distress associated with this word go down? Perhaps the word has lost some of its emotional impact, and the word is now just a word.

Exercise: Keep a Journal

Considerable research supports the benefits of disclosing painful situations in a journal for fifteen to thirty minutes a day. Describe in writing the facts about a difficult past event, particularly if you have never disclosed the event to anyone. For example, you might write "Mother yelled loudly at me when I broke the plate." Then record the associated thoughts and resulting feelings (such as "It seems unfair that she judged me. I can't bear it. I feel so sad and inept. I'm sorry that I disappointed her. I felt really clumsy and awkward. I started to feel that I'm no good when I make mistakes"). After keeping this type of journal for only a few days, people usually notice an improvement in their mood. They gain a sense of detachment and objectivity, and a feeling that they understand painful events better.

Exercise: Carry It with You

Write down all the "stuff" going on inside your head. You might draw a picture of a big head, and then write down all the negative thoughts and feelings that you carry. Alternatively, you might summarize in writing what you discovered in the two exercises above. Carry this summary around with you in a pocket for a day as a symbolic reminder that you can indeed bear the memories from the past and carry on with your life.

4

Be Aware of
Your Strengths

People with self-esteem are not necessarily brighter, more attractive, or more skillful than those who lack self-esteem. The difference really lies in the way we view ourselves. Dwelling on our negative aspects prevents us from enjoying our core worth and what is presently right about ourselves. Thinking "I can't like myself with this or that fault" also blocks self-acceptance, since it makes eliminating our faults a condition for worth. There will be a time to polish the rough edges and to grow. But for now let's focus on a more essential skill: doing an inventory of your strengths in order to view your core worth more accurately.

This chapter will help you to quietly do just that. The skills that we'll explore are not exercises in positive thinking. Rather, they are ways to try to see clearly and honestly what is already there. Recall our basic premise: each person already possesses in embryo every attribute needed to live well. The unique ways by which we express these strengths do not establish our worth—they remind us of our worth.

Let's consider creativity. Creativity is a wonderful strength that helps us invent useful devices, beautify our environment, and survive in a changing world. I often ask my students to raise their hand if they are creative. Typically only a few hands go up, because they narrowly define creativity as only an artistic talent; they think, in an all-or-nothing fashion, "Well, I'm not artistic so I must not be creative." I suggest that every person's hand could appropriately go up. Why? Because creativity can be expressed in many ways. Some people paint pictures and some sculpt. Others are creative in the way that they clean, cook, dress, bargain, amuse themselves, help others, make children laugh, tell stories, get themselves out of a jam, solve problems, organize, and so forth. Creativity is standard issue, but it can be expressed in many different ways, and it takes effort to develop dormant aspects of creativity.

Exercise: Regarding Your Core Worth

Imagine a crystal that represents core worth, with each facet representing a valued personality trait or attribute that all humans possess in various stages of development. Let's consider a list of these attributes:

Creativity

Flexibility (adapts to changing circumstances, can let go of a course of action that isn't working)

Wisdom (discernment, good judgment)

Humor, cheerfulness, playfulness

Character (ethics, integrity, honesty, fairness)

Kindness, compassion

Generosity

Respect for self

Respect and consideration for others

Patience

Self-acceptance

Openness, curiosity, awareness

Self-trust

Determination

Discipline

Courage

Humility

Gratitude

Optimism

Others: _____

On a sheet of paper, list the above attributes down the left side. Beside each, draw a scale that looks like this:

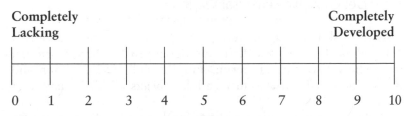

Next, rate each attribute in yourself from 0 to 10, where 10 means that the attribute is as well developed as it possibly could be in a person, and 0 means that the attribute is totally and completely lacking and is never demonstrated in the least degree. Try to simply notice the levels of these attributes without making negative judgments or comparisons. Remember, this is not a contest against others—because worth is equal and people express that worth in different ways and speeds. So try to be honest, neither inflating nor deflating your ratings.

Analysis

When you have finished, step back to see what has been revealed. If you are in touch with reality, you won't see a rating of 0 or 10, since you are neither perfect nor totally lacking in abilities. In this sense, we are all in the same boat. Each person is like a portrait in various stages of completion. Each person's portrait has a unique blend of colors. The light shines differently on each portrait, highlighting a different mix of strengths for each one. So while each person is infinitely worthwhile, each expresses that worth in an infinite variety of ways. You might take a few moments to record in a journal your thoughts and feelings about this exercise. As you consider your unique portrait, which areas do you most enjoy or find most satisfying?

Exercise: Cognitive Rehearsal Warm-up

This next skill is very effective and popular among individuals with whom I have worked. It was developed by three Canadian researchers (Gauthier, Pellerin, and Renaud 1983), who found that it increased self-esteem in adult subjects within a matter of weeks.

As a warm-up, place a check mark next to the appropriate traits or behavior below if you sometimes are or have been, to a reasonable extent, any of the following:

□ Friendly   □ Logical or reasonable

□ Calm or composed   □ Responsive to beauty or
                             nature

□ Flexible or adaptable   □ Brave

- ☐ Principled or ethical
- ☐ Expressive or articulate
- ☐ Fun loving or playful
- ☐ Organized, orderly, or neat
- ☐ Humorous, mirthful, or amusing
- ☐ Committed
- ☐ Loyal, dependable, or responsible
- ☐ Trustworthy
- ☐ Trusting or able to see the best in others
- ☐ Spontaneous
- ☐ Protective
- ☐ Caring or kind
- ☐ Conciliatory
- ☐ Dignified or graceful
- ☐ Open minded
- ☐ Imaginative
- ☐ Industrious

- ☐ Cooperative
- ☐ Sensitive, considerate, polite, or tactful
- ☐ Energetic, enthusiastic, or passionate
- ☐ Optimistic or hopeful
- ☐ Gentle
- ☐ Punctual
- ☐ Generous
- ☐ Adventurous
- ☐ Focused or disciplined
- ☐ Perceptive
- ☐ Affectionate
- ☐ Strong, powerful, forceful, or persuasive
- ☐ Resolute, determined, or persistent
- ☐ Patient
- ☐ Self-assured or self-confident
- ☐ Trusting of own instincts or intuitive
- ☐ Forgiving, or willing to look beyond faults and release bitterness

The list above represents personality traits or attributes. The list below contains various roles that we sometimes assume.

Check if you are sometimes reasonably good in any of the following roles:

- ☐ Listener
- ☐ Helper
- ☐ Decision maker
- ☐ Cook
- ☐ Cleaner
- ☐ Worker
- ☐ Friend
- ☐ Musician or singer
- ☐ Learner
- ☐ Leader or coach
- ☐ Follower
- ☐ Organizer
- ☐ Problem solver
- ☐ Handyperson
- ☐ Teacher
- ☐ Beautifier or designer
- ☐ Driver
- ☐ Letter writer
- ☐ Counselor
- ☐ Thinker
- ☐ Athlete

- ☐ Socializer
- ☐ Requester or advocate
- ☐ "Cheerleader" or supporter
- ☐ Example for others
- ☐ Planner
- ☐ Mate
- ☐ Taker of criticism
- ☐ Risk taker
- ☐ Enjoyer of hobbies
- ☐ Mistake corrector
- ☐ Smiler
- ☐ Debater
- ☐ Financial manager or budgeter
- ☐ Mediator
- ☐ Storyteller
- ☐ Family member
- ☐ Communicator
- ☐ Sibling
- ☐ Parent

Notice that when we remove the requirement for perfection we can better appreciate our strengths and the many things we *can* do. You are now ready to try the cognitive rehearsal exercise below.

Exercise: Cognitive Rehearsal

1. On a sheet of paper (or on index cards that you can slip into a pocket or purse), make a list of ten positive statements about yourself that are meaningful and true. The statements can come from the lists on the preceding pages and/or you can generate your own statements. You might write, for example, "I am a faithful and supportive member of my family," "I am disciplined," or "I am a concerned listener." If you mention a role that you perform well, try to add specific personal characteristics that explain why you do well in that role. For example, if you say that you are an effective manager, you might add that you plan thoroughly and treat people fairly. Roles can change (you might retire or be fired, for example), but you may express your character and personality traits across many different roles.

2. Find a place where you can relax without being disturbed for about twenty minutes. Reflect upon one statement and the evidence of its accuracy for one to two minutes. For example, if you noted in step 1 that you are a fair manager, you might reflect upon a recent decision you made in which people were treated equally. Repeat this for each statement.

3. Repeat this exercise every day for ten days. Each day, add an additional statement to your list, and reflect on the evidence of the accuracy of each of these statements as well.

4. Several times a day during the course of the ten days, look at an item on the list, and meditate for about two minutes on the evidence of its accuracy.

Cognitive rehearsal helps to counter the distortions that keep the focus on the negative, replacing them with appreciative thoughts and feelings. In a moment of clarity, Walt Whitman wrote, "I am larger, better than I thought. I did not think I held so much goodness" (Warner 2004, 142). Those who have tried this exercise have made similar statements, including the following:

- "Surprisingly, I felt calm and more in tune with myself."

- "I was pleased to see the amount of things I have going for me. It was an eye-opener."

- "I feel a sense of empowerment."

- "I felt a sense of negativity just lift away."

Exercise: The Goodness Within

Sharon Salzberg (2004) suggests an even simpler way to do this. Spend fifteen minutes remembering good or kind deeds that you have done, moments where you have been generous or caring, or times when you have lifted another person in some way, however small. Afterward, you might record your memories in a journal as a concrete reminder of the goodness within you.

5

Use Mindful Meditations

L ove is essential for mental health and self-esteem, and the lack of love seems to contribute to anxiety and low self-esteem. Young monkeys who do not bond with their mothers become very anxious. In humans, children who form loving bonds with their parents tend to demonstrate the benefits of self-esteem, and adult anxiety and low self-esteem are strongly associated with each other (Brown, Schiraldi, and Wrobleski 2003). In this chapter we will explore skills that help us to provide the healing love that might have been in short supply while we were developing. We will start by exploring mindfulness meditation approaches, and then introduce related skills that help us in this process.

Mindfulness

In one sense, mindfulness meditation is the experience of our true, happy, loving nature—the core self, known in the Tibetan view as the wisdom mind (see chapter 2).

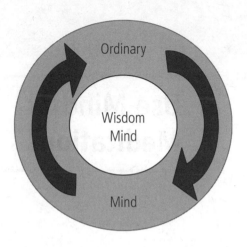

Figure 5

The battles that cause most of our suffering rage in the ordinary mind, where we become attached to racing negative thoughts and disturbing emotions, pulled away from our peaceful, kind center. The present moment becomes poisoned as we get ensnared and fatigued by these swirling, circling thoughts and feelings in the ordinary mind. The ordinary mind endlessly worries, plans, obsesses, remembers, regrets, evaluates, demands, criticizes, judges, protests, dramatizes, resents, questions, and hurries. It is said that we live in our heads while we miss out on life. And the more we struggle and protest against what we experience, the more aroused we become and the more we suffer.

There are three possible responses to distressing circumstances. We can fight, flee, or allow. When we fight, we tense up, and the tensing itself tends to increase arousal and pain. Cognitive therapy (CT; see chapter 3) focuses on replacing negative thoughts with more respectful, realistic thoughts, and in this way it helps us to be kinder to ourselves. We learn this in a rather active and effortful way. CT is a battle of sorts, albeit a useful one, whose very language exhorts us to punch back or fight back against those distortions. Another option·is to flee by avoiding, sedating, dissociating, wishing problems away, or asking why. None of these approaches is effective in the long run. Mindfulness uses the approach of allowing, which complements CT. Allowing, or accepting, means that we stop struggling with our challenges, and simply hold them in kind awareness. As we stop struggling and trying to fix problems, we gain a different perspective, an inner peace and confidence that we can handle life, and liberation from our attachments to negative thoughts and feelings.

Mindfulness meditations help us to go beneath the thoughts of the ordinary mind, which include the thoughts of self-dislike. As we do, we experience our core self—our true happy nature, or wisdom mind—whose natural state is compassionate, loving toward ourselves and others, vast, dignified, humble, clear, simple, peaceful, and whole. From the clear and vast perspective of the wisdom mind, we view thoughts simply as things that come and go, not who we really are at the core.

As one of my meditation teachers taught, we need not fight fear—we need only be aware of love. We need not create love—we need only be aware of what already exists inside. In mindfulness, we do not have to fight the thoughts of the ordinary mind. Instead, we greet them cordially, holding them with the loving-kindness and acceptance of the wisdom mind. As we become aware of the wisdom mind, it is as though its light breaks through the ordinary mind and unites with the light of truth beyond. The light of the wisdom mind penetrates, softens, or dissolves the intensity of our negative thoughts and feelings. Rather than fighting the negatives, we simply increase our experience with the positive emotions. As a result, the negatives tend to decrease.

What happens when we simply accept what is, without fighting or fleeing? Western medical research has found that mindfulness meditation reduces stress and mental and physical suffering. It also has been found to improve sleep and physical health, while increasing self-compassion and empathy for others. Mindfulness practices put us in touch with our loving core, who we really are—helping us to restore in us a sense of wholeness and allowing us to experience our inner strengths with clarity and love. We gain a sense of confidence from knowing that we can get beneath negative thoughts and not be controlled by them. Mindfulness reminds us that we are deeper than any dislike we experience on the surface.

Mindfulness also provides a way to take care of ourselves by accepting and soothing our distressing emotions, further increasing our self-confidence. After all, feelings are part of what makes us unique. If we try to judge and rid ourselves of our emotions, we are invalidating an important part of who we are. If we are more comfortable with our emotions, we become better able to stay calm and be more fully in contact with distressing situations. As a result, we respond more appropriately to crises and make better decisions, without emotional overreaction. People often say that mindfulness makes them feel more comfortable in their own skin.

Please remember that mindfulness does not try to fix or change situations immediately, but it does change the way we relate or respond to distressing thoughts and feelings. We simply allow them to be; we don't react with strong negative emotions, tension, bracing, judgments, impulsiveness, or the like. In mindfulness practice we simply watch calmly and with loving-kindness, viewing our thoughts and feelings from the dispassionate perspective of the wisdom mind. Later on, we might decide to try to change a situation from the strong position of full awareness. When we are open in this way, we become more open to the full range of feelings (all feelings are considered useful and treated the same), signals from our bodies (such as fatigue, pain, or true hunger as opposed to emotional hunger), our inner strengths and capacities, available choices when we are making a decision, and life's loveliness. We are likely to feel less exhausted as we detach from the battles in our ordinary mind.

So, in mindfulness, we simply pay attention to each moment fully, calmly, and kindly without trying to change anything right then. The attention is nonjudgmental because judging creates mental and physical arousal. (To say "I'm not good at meditation" or "I don't think it's working" is judging.) Instead, we have a welcoming, openhearted attitude when we practice. Rather than reacting emotionally, we respond always with loving-kindness.

Mindfulness-Based Stress Reduction Sequence

Jon Kabat-Zinn (1990; 2005) is known for introducing mindfulness-based stress reduction (MBSR) to Western medical circles in the late 1970s. Here, we will explore a simplified version of the eight-week program that he developed. Each form of meditation will build upon the previous form. So it will be important to practice each mindfulness meditation in turn. Kabat-Zinn has stressed the importance of practicing even when you don't feel like it. Why? With practice you will eventually be able to take in distressing thoughts, memories, emotions, and bodily sensations in the same calm way in which you might eat a raisin, which is where MBSR begins.

Exercise: The Raisins

The purpose of this exercise is to eat two raisins mindfully with full awareness over a ten- to fifteen-minute period.

1. Hold two raisins gently in the palm of your hand with a playful, curious attitude.

2. Pick one up and notice all the details of the raisin—the ridges, stem, translucence, color, and aroma. Notice the sensations in your fingers as you feel the surface of the raisin. Roll it between your fingers next to your ear and notice what that sounds like.

3. Notice your body as you hold it, noticing tension as you move it slowly toward your mouth. Sense the air against your skin as your hand moves slowly, much as you'd feel the water against your hand in the bath. Notice whether your body is signaling hunger. Pay attention to all the sensations in your hand and arm.

4. As you get ready to put it in your mouth, you might notice yourself thinking things like "I like [dislike] raisins. Mom used to give them to us for snacks. I'd like to eat lunch. I really don't have time to do this. There are probably a lot of calories in this raisin. What's this got to do with self-esteem?" This is good. Each time such thoughts arise, greet them cordially (thinking is what the ordinary mind does), and simply return your attention to eating the raisin.

5. Notice how your mouth accepts the raisin. As you let the raisin sit on your tongue, just sense it there and notice what it feels like before eating it. After a while place it on different areas of the tongue. Notice whether you salivate and taste the raisin.

6. Take a single bite and notice the flavor. You might notice a burst of flavor that is more intense than it seems when you mindlessly eat raisins.

7. Chew slowly, paying attention to what that feels like, and then notice the intent to swallow. As you swallow, follow the raisin down into your stomach. Notice the aftertaste and sensations in your body.

8. When you finish, do it again with the second raisin, being fully and calmly present for the experience.

Most of the elements of mindfulness are introduced in this exercise: being calmly present for an experience moment by moment without judging or emotionally reacting; being aware of the wandering mind, and gently escorting it back to the moment without judging; the beginner's mind (even though you might think all raisins are the same, eating the second raisin is not the same experience as eating the first); and realizing how much of life we miss when we are not mindful. Many notice that the experience of eating a raisin is more intense when the mind is focused on the present moment, and that they really notice flavors that they miss when they are in a hurry. Some say that they'd probably eat less if they were mindful because they'd enjoy each bite more and would notice when hunger signals had stopped.

Exercise: Mindful Breathing

This is a very effective meditation practice that helps us learn to be more peaceful in our own bodies, and to get under the racing thoughts in our heads. It takes about ten to fifteen minutes. Practice it once a day for a week.

1. Sit comfortably in the meditator's posture: Feet are flat on the floor; hands are resting, unfolded, comfortably in the lap, with palms up or down. The back is comfortably erect. Imagine that the spine is aligned like a column of golden coins resting one atop the other. The head is neither forward nor back; the chin is neither up nor down. The torso is held with dignity and grace, like a majestic mountain. The mountain is constant and secure, despite the clouds that cover it or the storms that batter it from without.

2. Allow your eyes to close. Release tension in the shoulders, neck, and jaw. Let the abdomen be soft and relaxed. Permit your body to relax and settle. Let yourself begin to settle in the wisdom mind.

3. Reflect on the attitudes of mindfulness for a moment— acceptance, loving-kindness, nonjudgment, patience, nonattachment, beginner's mind, humor, commitment, vastness, and generosity. In this meditation, you are not striving to make anything in particular happen. Just notice what occurs.

4. Let awareness go to your breathing, as you breathe abdominally (allow your upper body to be relaxed and still; the only movement is your abdomen rising as you breathe in and falling as you breathe out). Notice your breathing as you would watch waves flow in and out from the shore on the beach. As your breath is flowing, sense the parts of your body that are moving. You might sense the rising and stretching in your abdomen as you breathe in. You might notice the breath moving through your nostrils and throat and in and out of your lungs. Perhaps you notice your heart beating, slightly faster on the in breath and slightly slower on the out breath. Each breath is different, so pay attention to the entire breath with the beginner's mind.

5. As you breathe, thoughts will come and go. To fight them is to increase tension, so simply notice your mind wandering, and each time you notice that it has wandered, gently bring it back to focusing on breath. The object is not to stop yourself from thinking. Rather it is to feel satisfaction each time you notice your mind wandering. This is what the ordinary mind does. Congratulate yourself each time you mindfully notice this, and gently, kindly, patiently return your awareness to the breath without judging. Think of this as practice in responding to life with loving-kindness.

6. Release, relax, and rest in the breath. Notice fully each part of the in breath, the out breath, and each subtle, changing moment. Rest your mind in your belly, sensing what that is like.

7. And now feel the breath as if it were a wave that filled the entire body. Underneath the breath, notice a deeper calm, the peace within.

8. When you are finished, notice how you feel. Let that feeling go, just as you can let awareness of the breath come and go.

Exercise: Body Scan

We feel emotions and physical sensations in the body. Yet we often try to manage these in the head. We might think, "Oh, no. I don't want to feel that emotion. Not again. I've got to stop feeling that." Or, "This pain is terrible; I've got to find a way to kill it." The more we fight the feelings and sensations, the more we suffer. We are often quite out of touch with the body as we live in our heads, being more connected to television, computers, or cell phones than to our bodies. We might be obsessed with the image of our body in the mirror without being in tune with it, just as we may eat without really tasting. The body scan meditation will prepare us to eventually experience emotional and physical discomfort with kindness and calmness, without trying to push it away, run from it, or think ourselves out of it. This meditation teaches us to simply welcome in each sensation. We watch it kindly and dispassionately, and then let our awareness of the sensation dissolve. As we simply watch sensations, we notice that they often change; they come and go. When we do not tense up, but instead relax into the sensation, our response to the sensation changes. Many people observe that they feel grounded when they are centered in their bodies instead of their heads—peacefully observing the comings and goings of bodily sensations, and holding whatever comes up in calm awareness. The idea in this meditation is not to think about each region of the body, but to place your awareness deep inside it, feeling from inside. Practice this meditation for about forty minutes daily, for at least a week.

1. Lie down on your back in a place where you are unlikely to be disturbed. Close your eyes. Remember especially the attitudes of loving-kindness, patience, acceptance, non-judgment, letting go, and good humor.

2. Breathe and let your mind settle; let your mind rest calmly in your body.

3. Notice how your body as a whole feels at this moment without judging. Feel your skin against the carpet or bed. Notice the temperature of the air around you and how it feels. Be aware of how your body feels—is it comfortable, or is there any tension, pain, or itching? Notice the intensity of these sensations and whether they change or stay the same.

4. In a moment you will breathe in and out of one region of your body several times, paying full attention to all the sensations that you experience. It is as though your mind is resting in that area of the body. Then, when you are ready, you will release your awareness, letting awareness of that region dissolve as you also release tension in that area. Then you'll bring your awareness in a similar way to the next region. Each time your mind wanders, gently bring it back to the region on which you are focusing, without judging. Let's begin. We'll give directions starting with your left foot. Then we'll progress in a similar fashion to the other regions of the body.

5. Bring kind, openhearted attention to the toes of your left foot, letting your mind rest there. Imagine that you are breathing in and out of your toes. Perhaps you imagine air from your in breath flowing down through your nose, lungs, abdomen, and legs into your toes, and then, with your out breath, out from your toes, up through your body, and through your nose. Allow yourself to feel any and all sensations in the toes—pressure from a sock, temperature, blood flow, pulsing, relaxation, tension, and so on. Notice any changes in these sensations as you breathe. If you feel nothing, that is okay. Just notice whatever there is to experience without commenting or judging. When you are ready to leave this region, take a deeper and more intentional breath, following the breath down the toes once again. As you exhale, let awareness of the toes dissolve, releasing any tension or discomfort your body is willing to release at this time, as you bring awareness to the next region of your body (your left sole). Let your awareness stay in the next region in the same way for several breaths before moving on. As thoughts arise, silently say, "Thinking, thinking." Gently return your awareness to the region of the body and your breathing. Approach each region with the beginner's mind, as though you've never before paid attention to that

region. Watch whatever you experience without tensing or judging, but with kind, gentle, softhearted awareness. Repeat the process for each body part, following the list below:

Toes of left foot

Left sole

Left heel

Top of left foot

Left ankle

Left shin and calf

Left knee

Left thigh

Left side of groin

Left hip

Toes of right foot

Right sole

Right heel

Top of right foot

Right ankle

Right shin and calf

Right knee

Right thigh

Right side of groin

Right hip

Pelvic region, genitals, and buttocks

Lower back

Upper back

Spinal column

Stomach
Chest
Ribs
Heart
Lungs
Shoulder blades
Collarbones
Shoulders
Fingers of left hand
Left palm
Back of left hand
Left wrist
Left forearm
Left elbow
Left upper arm
Left armpit
Fingers of right hand
Right palm
Back of right hand
Right wrist
Right forearm
Right elbow
Right upper arm
Right armpit
Neck and throat (notice air flow)
Nose (notice air flow and smells without judgment)
Left ear
Right ear
Eyes

Cheeks

Forehead

Temples

Jaw and mouth

Face

Crown of head

6. Now be aware of your whole body, breathing in peaceful stillness. Go beneath your thoughts and feel the wholeness of the body. Notice what is moving or changing. Breathe through imaginary airholes in your head and feet. Breathe in through the head, following the breath down to the stomach, and, on the out breath, follow the breath down the legs and out the toes. Then breathe in through the feet, following the in breath to the stomach, and breathe out through the head. Ultimately feel your entire body breathing, like waves on the surface of the ocean, as you watch from the calm and peaceful depths.

Exercise: Smile Meditation

This beautiful meditation reminds us that happiness already exists within us as part of our true, happy nature. It is good to practice this at the beginning of the day and throughout the day. Allow about ten to fifteen minutes for this meditation.

1. Assume the meditator's posture, sitting comfortably erect, with feet flat on the floor and hands resting comfortably in the lap. The spine is straight like a column of golden coins. The upper body is relaxed but erect, sitting in graceful dignity like a majestic mountain. Allow your eyes to close. Let your breathing help you to settle into your restful wisdom mind.

2. Think of the playful, good-humored aspects of your true happy nature, or wisdom mind. Imagine for a moment what it would be like to smile. Perhaps you notice that just the idea of a smile tends to evoke feelings of being content, happy, relaxed, and softhearted. Just the thought of smiling relaxes and softens your face.

3. Now allow a genuine half smile to form on your face—perhaps a little twinkle that causes your eyes to sparkle, relaxing your face and jaw. The smile spreads across your face, bathing, soothing, and comforting your face.

4. Imagine that the smile spreads to the neck and throat, bringing happiness with it. Just sense happiness in that region, letting your mind rest there.

5. Now let happiness spread to the lungs; sense the comfort it brings to that area. Perhaps happiness feels like a warm light there. Whatever it is, just accept that and allow it to be.

6. Now let that feeling of happiness fill the heart, warming and soothing it. Breathe and let the mind rest there. Just allow happiness to settle in your heart.

7. Let the happy feeling of that smile spread to the stomach and any other areas of the body that you wish to focus on. Just sense the happiness in each region of the body.

8. Hold any thoughts that arise in kind friendliness, and return to experiencing the smile and happiness in the body. Conclude by sensing your whole body breathing and being comforted by the soothing, happy feeling of a smile.

Exercise: Sitting with Emotions

The meditation skills offered earlier in this chapter have prepared you for the following very powerful method of calming distressing emotions, and thereby taking care of yourself. This meditation teaches us to be calm and nonreactive in the presence of whatever emotions arise, good or bad.

The Tibetan master Sogyal Rinpoche (1993) teaches that the dragon, which represents our fears and pain, guards our greatest treasure. In other words, if we can overcome our tendency to flee from our fears and pain, then we can discover the deep reservoirs of peace and strength within. Chieko Okazaki (1993) relates the story of a Japanese village that had been terrorized by an unseen dragon, who roared from his cave in the nearby hills. One day, a little boy decided to approach the cave and invite the dragon to his birthday party. Despite the dragon's mighty roar and billowing smoke, the boy pleaded with the dragon to come. Eventually convinced that the boy was sincere, the dragon burst into tears. His tears were so voluminous that they created a river upon which the dragon and boy floated to the boy's home. Compassionate awareness changes things in a beautiful way.

The wisdom mind is indeed vast, loving, and accepting—wide and deep enough to hold any distressing emotion. Thus, we can be open to whatever exists, penetrating distressing emotions with healing, loving-kindness. Instead of fighting thoughts, memories, and feelings, we can learn to just embrace them, remembering compassion. It is like sitting with a beloved who is in pain, listening, and saying "Tell me about it. Whatever it is, it's okay." We listen without judging until the pain subsides and/or the person changes his response to the pain—relaxing rather than fighting it.

In this meditation, we learn to watch distressing emotions from the vast, detached perspective of the wisdom mind. The pain is impersonal; we don't identify with the pain ("There is pain," rather than "I have pain" or "I am the pain"). Remembering that the ordinary mind creates much suffering as we resist pain ("Why do I have to suffer? It's not fair. I can't stand this pain"), we change our response to pain by allowing the pain in. However, instead of bracing and tensing as we fight it, we relax into the pain with full acceptance. We don't judge emotions as bad or good; instead we accept both with equanimity, allowing love to penetrate and dissolve the pain. It is recommended that this meditation be practiced for thirty minutes or more each day for at least a week.

1. Assume the meditator's posture, sitting comfortably erect, with feet flat on the floor and hands resting comfortably in the lap. The spine is straight, like a column of golden coins. The upper body is relaxed but erect, sitting in graceful dignity like a majestic mountain. Allow your eyes to close. Let your breathing help you to settle into your peaceful wisdom mind.

2. Remember the key attitudes of acceptance, compassion, and nonjudgment. Remember that you are already whole. Use the beginner's mind as you explore a new way to experience feelings.

3. Be aware of your breathing for several minutes. Let your belly be soft and relaxed, watching it rise and fall as you breathe in and out, becoming still, peaceful, settled, grounded, and really present.

4. Be aware of any feeling in your body, any sensation as it comes and goes, without judging or trying to change it.

5. Whenever you find your mind wandering, congratulate yourself for noticing this. Remember that thoughts are not you, and bring your awareness gently back to breathing and sensing your body.

6. Recall a difficult situation, perhaps involving work or a relationship, and the related feelings of unworthiness, inadequacy, sadness, or worry about the future. Make a space for this situation. Give deep attention to these feelings. *Whatever* you are feeling is all right. Greet these feelings cordially, as you would greet an old friend.

7. Notice where in the body you feel the feelings (your stomach, chest, or throat, for example). Let yourself feel the feelings completely, with full acceptance. Don't think, "I'll tighten up and let these feelings in for a minute in order to get rid of them"—this is not full acceptance. Rather, create a space that allows the feelings to be completely accepted.

8. Breathe into that region of the body with great love, as if fresh air and sunlight were entering a long-ignored and darkened room. Follow your breath all the way down through the nose, throat, lungs, and then to the part of the body where you sense the distressing emotion(s). Then follow the breath out of your body, until you find yourself settling. You might think of a kind, loving, accepting smile as you do this. Don't try to change or push the discomfort away. Don't brace or struggle with it. Just embrace it

without judging it, with real acceptance, deep attention, loving-kindness, and peace. Let the body soften and open around that area. The wisdom mind is vast enough to hold these feelings with great compassion; love is big enough to embrace, welcome, and penetrate the discomfort. Let your breath caress and soothe the feelings as you would your adored sleeping baby.

9. View the discomfort from the dispassionate perspective of the wisdom mind. It is as if you are watching waves of discomfort rise on the surface of the ocean, and then be reabsorbed into the vast ocean. The waves come and go without changing the basic nature of the ocean. If you find it helpful, you might think of loved ones who remind you of loving-kindness and let that loving kindness penetrate your awareness as you remember that difficult situation. Simply notice what happens to the feelings without trying to make them change.

10. When you are ready, take a deeper breath into that area of the body and, as you exhale, widen your focus to your body as a whole. Pay attention to your whole body's breathing, being aware of the wholeness and the vast, unlimited compassion of the wisdom mind that will hold any pain that comes and goes. Your attention now expands to the sounds you are hearing, just bringing them into awareness without commenting or judging. Simply listen with a half smile. Feel the air against your body; sense your whole body breathing. Notice all that you are aware of with a soft and open heart.

11. To conclude, say the following intentions silently to yourself: "May I remember loving-kindness. May I be happy. May I be whole."

So long as one is a human being ... self-love should be there.

—Dalai Lama

Mindfulness-Based Cognitive Therapy

From cognitive therapy (CT) we learn a useful way for dealing with the drama that plays out in the ordinary mind: we first become aware of our distorted automatic thoughts and then replace these with more constructive thoughts. This tends to reduce the severity of the disturbing emotions that we experience. Further relief can be gained by becoming aware of and replacing our inaccurate core beliefs. In chapter 3 we used the example of failing a promotion test. This situation triggered various unreasonable negative thoughts, which resulted in feelings of depression and anxiety. One such thought was "I'll fail the retest. It will be awful." Replacing such thoughts with more logical thoughts ("If I prepare more effectively, I might pass") reduces distress somewhat. In CT, the person is asked a series of questions that are designed to help him or her uncover the core belief, such as "Why would failing the retest be so bad?" and "What would that mean about you?" Such questions uncover the so-called core belief, which is then challenged and replaced. For example, a person might reply that failing the retest would prove that he is inadequate. The faulty logic of this core belief is challenged (for example, "I am clearly not always and in every way inadequate"), thus providing additional relief.

Core beliefs are often learned early in life. They often take the following forms:

- "I am inadequate [weak, incompetent, help-less, out of control, not capable enough, no good]."

- "I am unlovable [unlikable, unwanted, reject-able, different, bad]." (Beck 1995)

Even though they are called "core beliefs," these do not accurately reflect the core; they are only thoughts in the ordinary mind. Because they were acquired early in life, they are accompanied by strong feelings that are difficult to reason away. Logic does not entirely soothe the feelings. Who has not felt genuinely inadequate or unlovable at times? One woman said, "When I wake up all disheveled and grouchy, you can't tell me I'm lovable." As the Zen master Seng-Ts'an said, "If you work on your mind with your mind, how can you avoid great confusion?" (Hayes, Strosahl, and Wilson 1999, 12). We might restate this by saying, "Thinking alone is usually insufficient to heal deeply held beliefs and feelings."

Sadly, a "hardened" criminal once exclaimed, "Don't you understand that a criminal is who I am!" He had not softened to the possibility that his perception of his identity was just a thought. He had attached to the ordinary mind's thought as if it were ultimate truth, letting the thought drive his behavior and self-concept—thus blocking change. Core beliefs have a way of getting entrenched in the ordinary mind. They are difficult to uproot with logic alone.

Mindfulness-based cognitive therapy (MBCT; Segal, Williams, and Teasdale 2002; McQuaid and Carmona 2004) brings the heart back into the picture, giving a complementary way to handle upsetting thoughts and feelings. This approach focuses mainly on the feelings (of being unlovable, inadequate, and so on). Instead of fighting the distorted thoughts, we learn to accept the thoughts and feelings, letting their intensity dissolve as we sit with them with loving-kindness—viewing them from the nonjudgmental perspective of the wisdom mind. We disengage from rumination, going under the thoughts and holding the feelings with the compassion of a soft heart until they soften.

Some feel that the approach below provides an easier, more natural way to get to the core beliefs. Try this several times over the course of the next week, until you feel comfortable with the skill. (See the example at figure 6, below.)

1. Identify a difficult situation that triggered upsetting feelings. Write it down. Underneath it, describe and rate the intensity of the resulting feelings.

2. In the first of two columns, write down your automatic thoughts, without judging them. Just breathe, and, with a dispassionate view, write them down.

3. In the second column, write down a mindful response for each automatic thought. Mindful responses are brief phrases or sentences that reflect acceptance and kindness without trying to change the automatic thoughts. The following examples might help you select suitable responses:

"Thinking that ..."

"It's just a thought."

"Believing the thought that ..."

"Accepting this thought ..."

"Nonjudging."

"That's the way it is." (This is excellent for "should" statements, such as "I should have known better" or "I shouldn't be this way.")

"It's okay (smiling, just holding that thought in kind awareness)."

"This is difficult. Remember loving-kindness. Love is deeper than this thought."

"Feeling compassion ..."

"Breathing, letting that thought settle in the body ..."

"Holding this thought softly in awareness ..."

"Remembering patience and nonstriving ..."

"Just sitting with this thought and emotion ..."

"Holding this fear with compassion ... it's okay to be afraid."

"Accepting disappointment ..."

"Beginner's mind ..." (This is especially useful when we think "I can't do this" or "I'm a loser.")

Accepting that thought, then letting it go."

4. Sit with each automatic thought for a few moments without trying to modify it. Notice what feelings and sensations each thought triggers in your body. Breathe into this with loving-kindness, without judging the thoughts or feelings, reacting emotionally, or fighting them, as you hold in awareness the mindful response to each automatic thought. Notice if the intensity of the thoughts or feelings changes as you watch them from the perspective of the wisdom mind.

Figure 6

MBCT Double-Column Technique

Difficult Situation: My computer freezes as I'm working on an important project at home at night.

Resulting Feeling(s)	Initial Ratings	Rating After Sitting with the Core Belief
Angry	8	6
Frustrated	7	5

Automatic Thoughts	Mindful Response
I can't stand it when this happens.	Having the thought that I can't stand this
It should do what I paid it to do.	It is what it is—accepting
I must meet the deadline.	Breathing; accepting that this is difficult
I must excel.	Believing the thought that I must excel

5. Uncover the core belief. Regarding the distressing situation, you can ask yourself questions, such as "Why is this so bad?" "What's the worst thing about this?" "What does this mean about me?" and "What is the deepest hurt or fear?" Perhaps it is the fear that you are inadequate, or the feeling that you are alone, unable to get needed help, as you felt when you were a child. In our example, you might realize that you could miss the boss's deadline because your computer is malfunctioning, that the boss might criticize you, and that you might react by thinking (and feeling) that you are inadequate—which is the core belief.

6. Sit with the core belief (and feeling) as you learned to do in the Sitting with Emotions exercise above. That is, notice the feeling without judging or reacting emotionally. Hold it in the body, kindly penetrating it with soothing loving-kindness until the core belief and associated feeling begin to soften in intensity. Remember the dignity and immeasurable worth of each individual.

7. Rerate the original feelings in figure 6. Notice how these might have lessened in intensity.

Notice that MBCT does not change the situation; it only changes our response to the situation. It teaches us to lessen the intensity of our emotional reactions so that we can function at our best.

Exercise: Time Tripping

This strategy helps us to touch our past selves with love, helping to soften painful experiences from long ago that might have resulted in feelings of inadequacy, rejection, powerlessness, shame, loneliness, or the like. Allow about thirty minutes for this exercise.

1. In a place where you won't be disturbed, sit in the meditator's posture, with feet flat on the floor, and hands resting comfortably in the lap. The spine is straight, like a column of golden coins. The upper body is relaxed but comfortably erect, sitting in graceful dignity like a majestic mountain. Allow your eyes to close. Let your breathing help you to settle into your restful wisdom mind.

2. Think of a painful experience from your past. Call the person experiencing the painful experience your "younger self." Your present self, the "wiser self," understands the healing power of compassion and has greater skill and experience than the younger self had.

3. Imagine that the wiser self goes back in time to visit the younger self during that difficult time. The wiser self cherishes the core of the younger self and knows that the mistreatment or mistake that the younger self has experienced is not who the younger self is at the core. By the kind way that the wiser self looks, speaks, and/or touches the younger self, he or she helps the younger self feel secure, protected, and loved. From the perspective of experience, the wiser self senses and provides what the younger self needed at that time, whether it be encouragement, physical protection, counsel, hope, an embrace, a wink, or soothing words. The younger self accepts this kindness, resting in it. Sense this happening.

Exercise: The Mindful Mirror

Try this practice each time you see yourself in the mirror over the next few days.

Look directly and deeply into your eyes with genuine and heartfelt loving-kindness. Look beyond the wrinkles or blemishes. If you notice stress in your eyes, try to acknowledge and understand that, and let the stress dissolve. Continue to look into your eyes, perhaps with a kind half smile and a feeling of welcoming acceptance and good humor, touching the core with loving-kindness.

It is usually not thinking, or even time, that heals, but love.

—Anonymous

6

Cultivate Joy

L ife is difficult, and one of life's greatest challenges is how to enjoy it. Cultivating more joy in life promotes self-esteem by building our confidence in our ability to experience mastery and pleasure. Creating space for recreative enjoyment is also a way of taking care of ourselves. Since self-esteem and happiness are strongly correlated (Brown, Schiraldi, and Wrobleski 2003), and because increasing happiness likely raises self-esteem, this chapter focuses on ways to increase happiness and wholesome pleasure.

Although happiness is a more enduring and steady condition than pleasure, activities that promote wholesome pleasure (activities that consider the well-being of self and others and do no harm) are also beneficial. For example, studies have shown that simply increasing pleasant events can elevate mood as effectively as trying to eliminate distortions (Jacobson and Christensen 1996). Before exploring the approaches to increasing happiness and wholesome pleasure, let's examine the factors that can undermine our efforts.

Happiness Myths

Certain myths, which can be readily challenged, appear to reduce one's ability to enjoy life:

- **I must have wealth in order to enjoy life.** Once a person's income rises above the poverty level, the amount of money they have bears little relation to their happiness. In fact, people tend to be happier when their entertainment is inexpensive and requires their active participation. Thus, it is not surprising that passive entertainment like watching television tends to lower people's mood. Greater benefits tend to result from immersion in activities that require investment of one's strengths, such as reading or helping others.

- **Playing is somehow immature or wrong.** As Gandhi taught, it is not pleasure, but pleasure without conscience, that corrupts consciousness. Wholesome pleasure improves happiness and productivity.

- **All work must be completed before pleasure is experienced.** Taken to its illogical extreme, this myth would prevent everyone from having pleasure, since there is always more work that could be done.

- **Only the outcome matters; the process does not.** The process is a journey that can be enjoyed. The trick is to find satisfaction in our work and in the other aspects of life. Does it do us any good to be rich in achievements but impoverished in joy?

- **I must "succeed" to have worth; my worth when playing is less than my worth when producing.** This statement erroneously equates market worth with inner worth. Inner worth is the same whether we are sleeping, playing, or producing.

- **Pleasure decreases productivity.** Certainly one can overdo pleasure or use it to escape life's responsibilities. However, happy people tend to be more productive and make better decisions than unhappy people.

- **My mistakes and flaws disqualify me from deserving pleasure.** Mistakes and flaws make us fallible but never undeserving or worthless at the core.

- **With all the depression and problems in the world, it's nearly impossible to be happy.** In fact, most people are generally happy, irrespective of gender, race, age, employment status, and even mental and physical handicaps.

- **I must be attractive to be happy.** Happiness is an inside job and is relatively independent of appearance.

Success is being happy. Happiness is loving yourself, loving others, and getting to do the things that you love. I love to rock climb, surf, and paint, to name a few.

—Mike Dolan, former student

A Thorough Medical or Psychological Evaluation

In a moment, we'll discuss strategies for increasing happiness and wholesome pleasure. In general, however, it's helpful to first treat conditions that can degrade one's mood and ability to experience pleasure, some of which are listed below:

- **Common mental illnesses, such as depression, anxiety, and problem anger,** are associated with unhappiness. One type of anxiety disorder, **post-traumatic stress disorder (PTSD),** can result from abuse; rape; combat; industrial or traffic accidents; crime; terrorism; torture; and police, firefighting, and other emergency service work.

- **Thyroid imbalance** is called the "great mimic," because it can cause depression, anxiety, premenstrual symptoms, old-age memory loss, elevated cholesterol levels, weight gain, and many other symptoms affecting the mind and body.

- **Sleep apnea** is characterized by snoring that stops and starts frequently throughout the night. This condition can cause oxygen deprivation, leading one to feel depressed, fatigued, and sexually disinterested. It is also a risk factor for headaches, heart attacks, high blood pressure, and strokes.

- **Elevated cholesterol** can sometimes cause depression, as can diabetes.

All of these conditions can be successfully treated or managed with the proper medical or psychological help. A thyroid stimulating hormone (TSH) test can detect thyroid problems that normal blood tests sometimes miss. A variety of stress management strategies can be used in conjunction with the treatment of a number of these problems. These strategies include abdominal breathing, systematic relaxation, exercise, nutrition, sleep hygiene, time management, and interpersonal or communication skills. Quitting smoking can also reduce stress and mood fluctuations. PTSD is best treated by a specially trained trauma specialist (see Recommended Resources at the end of the book).

Everyday Mindfulness

Mindfulness helps us to be fully present in the moment, without letting our racing thoughts (worries, plans, judgments, and so on) pull us out of the moment. Everyday mindfulness carries the benefits of mindfulness meditation, which is a way of being calm and joyful (see chapter 5). Over the next few days, select at least one activity to experience mindfully (see the list of suggestions below). Use your breathing to settle your mind in your body as you just watch and enjoy all of the aspects of the activity. As you breathe, allow yourself to rest in your wisdom mind, feeling serene and at ease. Perhaps you smile slightly as you relax into the present moment, knowing that each moment can be peaceful and beautiful. When a thought intrudes, just notice the thought with a cordial attitude and gently bring your full attention back to the activity. Simply experience the event fully, noticing the things we so often miss in our hurried lives. Go slowly and take in all of the sensations—tastes, sights, aromas, sounds, textures—and notice how your body feels before, while, and after you do the activity. Try to only do the activity, focusing on nothing else. Watch from the perspective of the compassionate wisdom mind. You might select an activity to try from the following list:

- Watch something in nature, such as clouds, rain, stars, the moon, a flower, or a tree.

- Eat a meal.

- Drive your car.

- Wash the car.

- Brush your teeth.

- Take a shower or bath.

- Wash your hands.

- Wash dishes.

- Walk. (Feel each sensation in your legs as you mindfully move and your feet meet the ground.)

- Sit in the sun.

- Truly listen to someone (without judging or thinking of what you are going to say; notice what your body feels and what is in your heart; try to discern what the person feels in his or her heart).

- Hold a baby.

- Get in bed.

- Do a hobby.

- Play a children's game.

- Exercise.

- Listen to or tell a joke. (Notice how it feels to be amused.)

- Plan spontaneity. (You might set aside a day for recreation with only general plans, such as going to the zoo or driving through the country, and just enjoy whatever develops. This can be done alone or with a partner.)

No one can live without delight, and that is why a man deprived of joy of spirit goes over into carnal pleasures.

—St. Thomas Aquinas

Gratitude

Happy people tend to be grateful. The pessimist tends to look at a glass of water that is half full and thinks, "Why is it only half full? Why can't it be completely full?" The happy person thinks, "What beautiful, clear water." Again, mindfulness helps us. Eastern spiritual masters teach that we can be content in any given circumstance, even as we might try to improve it. At the same time, attachment causes unhappiness. If we demand money, looks, possessions, titles, or a particular way of being treated by others, then these things are controlling our happiness. If you insist upon having a particular prestigious position, for example, then how will you feel if you don't have it or can't get it? If you do have it, you might worry that you'll be fired. If your authority is challenged, then you might become angry. Gratitude, however, permits us to celebrate all that we enjoy, becoming attached neither to the things we possess nor to the things we lack. Thus, one can enjoy watching the clouds from a mansion, a hut, or a prison.

Below are a few other ideas for experiencing more gratitude:

- Try keeping a gratitude journal. Each day record three or four things for which you have felt grateful over the last twenty-four-hour period. See if your mood has improved after a week or so. If it has, keep writing in the gratitude journal.

- Think of people who have made a difference in your life. You might wish to express heart-felt gratitude to these people in a phone call or a note.

- Finally, play the reminiscing game with friends or loved ones. Here, you simply say, "Remember when we did such and such. Wasn't that fun? Didn't we laugh?"

How much money does it take for one to be happy? A little bit more than he's got.

—John D. Rockefeller

Sentence Stem Completion

Another way to approach pleasant events is the sentence stem completion activity. This strategy asks you to respond as fast as you can, without thinking or worrying about the practicality of your answers. The assumption is that the ideas that matter most are already inside us and will come out spontaneously. You can try this with just one other person or several people sitting in a circle. Each person states the first sentence stem aloud and then completes it with the first idea that comes to mind. Continue until the ideas for that sentence stem have run out, and then move on to the next sentence stem. If you are trying this strategy alone, simply write down your responses, one after another, on a sheet of paper. Try these sentence stems:

> *What occupied and amused me as a child was ...*
>
> *My idea of a good time is ...*
>
> *My idea of a simple pleasure is ...*
>
> *Something I did as a child that I would still enjoy is ...*

This strategy is a very enjoyable way to stimulate creative thinking. One man, who had grown up in a diplomat's family, surprised me by saying that his idea of a good time was reading the newspaper on the stoop. (Somehow I thought he would say something like going to the opera or a famous museum.) When I first began using this strategy, I started to think about the simple pleasures that I had enjoyed as a child and could still enjoy, such as climbing a tree or playing children's games. So I suggested that my family play Red Light, Green Light at family gatherings, and we did so until the children got too old. I was a bit sad that I couldn't convince the adults to keep playing anyway, because we had had so many hearty laughs. But I still continue to reclaim some simple pleasures from childhood, such as shooting arrows into the air with the same bow I used to play with as a child.

Traditions

A tradition is anything that is enjoyed and repeated; it is a return to the comfortable and familiar. It is also what we lose, along with some of our humanity, when we become too busy and have little extra time. Most people have a treasured tradition or two. Many of these can be preserved or reinstituted. For some the tradition might be a holiday celebration. For others, traditions can be simple, such as a sit-down dinner on Sunday evenings. (One woman said her Mother's Day tradition was to go to any restaurant where she didn't have to "look up to see the menu.") Some couples reserve Friday evenings for date nights, and some families set aside one night a week for playing games together, telling uplifting stories, and sharing a dessert. A tradition might also mean working together as a family, or designating an evening as a time for being with friends, since we tend to lose friends when we become too busy for them.

Mastery and Competence Imagery

Pat yourself on the back if you have made it this far in life and have managed to preserve a reasonable degree of sanity. Can you remember a time in your life when you confronted a challenge and handled it well, even though it was difficult? You might think of mastering difficult material in school, performing a complicated work of music or doing well in an athletic competition, resolving a conflict with another person, or being afraid but persisting anyway. Do you remember how good this felt? In order to survive, we've each had to master certain challenges. Take a few moments to identify some of these moments. Jot them down on a piece of paper. Now take a few moments to focus on one of these experiences, perhaps the one that you feel best about. We'll call this your "mastery and competence image." Assume your meditator's posture— feet flat on the floor, back comfortably erect, hands resting in the lap—and relax in your breath. Imagine the experience in detail—what you did, thought, felt, saw, heard, and sensed in your body. Take your time, recalling the details until the experience becomes vivid in your imagination. Then record all of these details in a notebook or on a piece of paper (writing them down helps the details to become more vivid and concrete). This is your mastery and competence image. Because this imagery is drawn from your real-life experience, this exercise evokes powerful feelings of confidence and satisfaction that tend to replace negative feelings and boost self-esteem.

Next, identify an upcoming situation that you associate with anxiety—perhaps taking a test, negotiating a raise with the boss, or tackling a difficult assignment. Break the situation down into a hierarchy of ten to twenty steps, from the least difficult aspect of the situation to the most difficult. (Alternatively, your hierarchy can break the feared event into ten to twenty chronological steps.) After completing the hierarchy, sit in the meditator's posture. Think of the least distressing step on the hierarchy (or the first step, if your hierarchy is chronological), allowing yourself to fully feel with an open heart any distress that is associated with that step for a few moments. Relax in your breathing. Notice where you feel distress in your body and breathe into that area with compassion. Now bring into awareness your mastery and competence image. Fully and completely experience all of the details of this image. After you see this image vividly in your mind, imagine that all of the thoughts, feelings, and sensations in your mastery and competence image fully penetrate that distressing step on the hierarchy. Stay with this for a few moments until you feel a shift in the feelings associated with the distressing step.

Repeat this cycle of allowing in the distress and then penetrating it with your mastery and competence image a few times until you feel that you can experience this step on the hierarchy with relatively little distress. Then progress to the next step on the hierarchy and repeat the procedure. Eventually, after you've transferred feelings of mastery and competence to each step on the hierarchy, you'll experience the distressing event in a calmer, more confident way.

As time permits, call to mind other mastery and competence images. Describe them in your notebook and make them a part of your coping repertoire.

Sense of Humor

Humor is universally valued and used by resilient survivors. But it's much more than telling jokes. Humor is about having a kind and playful outlook on life—it pleasantly brings us back to our wisdom mind and helps us to realize that mishaps are not who we are. Thus, humor affords a presence of mind and a sense of equanimity in the face of our mistakes. It is about acceptance, optimism, and clarity. It enables us to say, "You know, I'm not perfect, but I'm a darn sight better than some might think." As one elegant woman I know once said, "We have to laugh at ourselves because we all do ridiculous things sometimes."

Humor helps us endure adversity, making the sour seem bittersweet, providing comic relief, and lightening things up. When we find something to laugh about despite the absurdities of life, we are saying "I can figure a way to rise above even this, at least temporarily; things could be worse."

A shared laugh brings people together and reminds us that we are not alone in our misery. The World War II concentration camp survivor Viktor Frankl (1959) told of two prisoners who joked about how prison camp lessons could transfer to real life: they visualized going to a dinner party after the war and asking that their soup be ladled from the bottom. During that war, Irene Gut Opdyke hid twelve Jews in the basement of a villa while she kept house for a German major upstairs (I. G. Opdyke, personal communication). Despite the grave danger they were in, she said, they all thought it funny, even farcical, to think that they were stealing food from beneath the commandant's nose. Another example of the power of humor took place during the frightful Battle of the Bulge, when surrounded GIs maintained strict roadblocks. An American officer approached one roadblock in a jeep driven by an African-American, but the officer didn't know the password. He impatiently reached for his pistol as he demanded to pass. Eight sentries clicked the safeties of their rifles as they prepared to fire. At that tense moment, the driver exclaimed, "Oh, man, you know I ain't no Nazi!" The affection and respect with which this story was told suggested that laughter helped to break down the walls separating people as it broke up the tension of the moment (R. B. Jacobs, personal communication).

You might find it helpful to remember the following principles when cultivating a sense of humor:

- **Keep humor affectionate and playful, and good-natured rather than hostile.** Wholesome humor allows us to share our common lot and faults in life. There is a sense that we're all in this together. Avoid sarcasm and ridicule, which can separate people. Think of humor as an act of service that can lift people's spirits if used kindly.

- **We don't have to try to be funny.** Just notice or describe life's incongruities, and have the courage to laugh.

- **Be yourself.** You can either give humor away (jokes, pranks, good-natured ribbing, endearing nicknames) or you can absorb or appreciate humor (noticing the ridiculous, chuckling at mistakes, laughing with others). You can be low key, dry, or boisterous. You might find that you are funny around close friends, but not in large groups. All of these approaches are okay.

- **Be flexible.** Overusing humor can be a form of escapism and avoidance of genuine feelings. There are times when it is insensitive or inappropriate to laugh. If you are unsure about your use of humor in a particular situation, check it out. Explain that you were trying to lighten things up, and ask if it was all right with the people around you.

- **Try noticing the joyful aspects of life before trying to be funny** ("Did you see that beautiful moon?"). If you can then make another person laugh, that's icing on the cake.

Attitudes Toward Suffering

Life is indeed difficult. Whining, complaining, second-guessing or pitying ourselves, cursing life, and blaming keep us feeling powerless and angry, which only increases our suffering. Those who successfully survive adversity develop a different way to view suffering. For example, prisoners of war learn to acknowledge the internal wounds that they've suffered, but they also realize that their adversity revealed strengths that they otherwise would not have discovered. Sometimes adversity teaches us that we can endure more than we assumed we could, or it forces us to develop persistence and determination. Suffering can lead to greater empathy and new purpose, inspiring us to help others. It can also help us to appreciate the simple pleasures in life. And watching others endure suffering with dignity can help us appreciate the character within others. Most resilient survivors would not wish to relive the difficult periods in their lives, yet most say they would not trade past challenges for the lessons they've taught. Rather than wincing or trying to avoid pain, we can learn to courageously turn into the wind of adversity and seek pain's tutorials.

Cultivate Optimism

Optimism is another correlate of happiness, self-esteem, and resilience. Optimism is not the unrealistic expectation that everything will turn out well—that would be overconfidence, which can lead to disappointment and poor performance. Rather, optimism is the attitude that helps us say:

- "If I try, things are likely to turn out as well as possible."

- "No matter how bad things become, I can find something to enjoy."

- "If things don't turn out well in one area, other areas are likely to turn out well."

- "'Bad luck' is not permanent, so I can approach things with an open, beginner's mind."

The following strategies can help us to cultivate optimism:

- When something does not turn out well, think like an optimist. Optimists live longer and have better mental and physical health than pessimists. They also perform better than pessimists in the workplace. A pessimist thinks (1) "Something is wrong with me at the core"; (2) "Everything goes wrong like this"; and (3) "Things will never improve." An optimist, by contrast, thinks: (1) "This was a difficult *situation*"; (2) "I do other things well"; and (3) "Things will likely improve."

- Read about people such as Viktor Frankl or Arthur Ashe who endured suffering with optimism (see Recommended Resources).

- When something goes awry, practice the "at least" exercise: "I lost my home, but at least I still have my family"; "I lost my job, but at least I don't have to tolerate my boss anymore"; "From this adversity, at least I learned that I can endure great difficulty." (The last example demonstrates "survivor's pride," the confidence and strength that one gains from enduring tragedy or hardship.)

7

Appreciate Your Body

Have you ever noticed what you see when you look in the mirror? Do you view your overall appearance and countenance cordially and kindly, or do you home right in on your body's flaws? One approach leads to a satisfying feeling; the other results in a feeling of disappointment.

The body is an external. Our inner worth is not related to our weight, appearance, or health status (although our culture might lead us to believe otherwise). However, the way we experience our body typically corresponds to the way we experience our core selves. If we reject our bodies overall because of particular perceived flaws, we are also likely to condemn our core selves for some present imperfections. If our bodies have been mistreated, ridiculed, or called names, we may learn to experience our bodies with shame. By extension, this shame might spread to the core self. Yet we can learn to experience our bodies with greater appreciation and satisfaction. This in turn helps us to adopt a more accepting attitude toward our inner selves.

The media could lead us to believe that one could not possibly be happy if one is physically imperfect. Nevertheless, a fascinating story appeared on *20/20 Downtown* about Kevin Miller, a beloved music teacher who happened to weigh six hundred pounds (Miller 2000). With the help of his loving wife, Miller learned that his identity rests inside him. He learned to accept himself while trying every day to manage his weight. As a result, his students learned to look beneath superficial, outer appearances. Likewise, when Christopher Reeve of *Superman* fame became paralyzed, his wife told him that she would understand if he wanted to end his life, but that she still loved him and hoped that he would choose to live. His child, understanding the difference between core worth and externals, said that his father could no longer run, but he could still smile. So the immeasurable worth of the core persists, despite the imperfections of the body. Just as we can learn to accept our core worth as different from our externals, we can also learn to appreciate our bodies, despite their imperfections. Let's see how this is done.

Consider the Magnificence of the Body

It is easy to contemplate the magnificence of a mountain peak, a field of wheat, a tall building, the ocean at sunset, a stallion galloping across the plains, a single flower, or a piece of fruit. Let's also take a moment to ponder the breathtaking complexities of the body.

Each of our cells contains the genetic plan for producing all of the cells in our bodies. The genetic code contains billions of steps of DNA that would extend more than five feet in length if stretched out in a line. However, this code is coiled to a length of only 1/2500 of an inch within the nucleus of each cell. From this single blueprint, cells divide and specialize, such that some cells become cells of the heart, others become cells of the eye, nerves, or bones, and so on. The trillions of cells in the body, millions of which are replaced each second, would stretch over a million miles if placed end to end.

The blood vessels of the body stretch over 75,000 miles. The heart consists of two muscle pumps, one strong enough to cause blood to course through these many miles of vessels, the other gentle enough to move blood through the lungs without bursting the delicate air sacs found there. The heart, weighing just eleven ounces, beats tirelessly, each day pumping enough blood to fill several railroad cars. Tissue-thin valves of the heart usually work flawlessly, without ever pausing, over the course of an entire lifetime.

The 206 bones of the body are stronger, ounce for ounce, than steel or reinforced concrete. Science cannot duplicate the durability and flexibility of a joint like the thumb, which requires thousands of messages from the brain to direct its complex movements.

The complicated neural circuitries of the eyes, ears, and nose enable us to distinguish thousands of colors, sounds, and smells, while the ear and brain work together to detect the slightest postural imbalance. Under the skin, an area the size of a fingernail contains hundreds of nerve endings that detect touch, temperature, and pain; scores of sweat glands to cool the body; and numerous melanocytes to defend against the sun's rays. The skin can detect and distinguish the sensations of a hug, a massage, or a pleasant breeze, increasing our capacity for pleasure.

The immune system of the body is more complex than the most sophisticated army. The salty, acidic skin prevents many impurities from entering the body. The nose, airways, and lungs work together to filter, humidify, and regulate temperature of incoming air. Lysozyme in the nose and acids in the stomach destroy potent incoming microbes, while billions of specialized white blood cells work together to neutralize microbes that enter the body. And the white blood cells remember the markers of microbes they've encountered so that they can efficiently destroy them in the future.

The immune system is regulated by the brain, through a complex dance of nerves and hormones, which allows affirmative emotions such as love and hope to sometimes strengthen the immune system. The brain, weighing in at three pounds, contains one hundred billion nerve cells and is more complex than any computer. The brain continuously monitors the body and then initiates needed adjustments in temperature, blood sugar, fluid balance, and blood pressure. In addition to permitting logical thinking, the brain allows us to recognize unique faces, understand subtle facial and vocal expressions, mobilize to fight or flee when we are threatened, remember vital lessons, and set goals.

Finally, the body is able to convert ingested food to needed energy, and it has a remarkable capacity to repair itself.

Exercise: A Simple Body Appreciation Activity

As often as you can, stand briefly in front of a mirror or look directly at your body. Instead of noticing what's wrong (such as a blemish, bags under your eyes, or wrinkles), notice what is right, what is working. Pay attention to your hair, your clean skin, your ability to stand and move, or the color of your eyes. You might consider the wonders described above. If you are stumped, simply move your thumb around and notice the marvelous complexities and varied movements that are possible. Then expand your awareness to other marvels of the body, outside and in.

Exercise: Body Appreciation Meditation

This meditation, developed by Jack Canfield in 1985, is a very effective way to cultivate body appreciation. It is practiced once a day over about a thirty-minute period and is especially effective when practiced repeatedly. Sit or lie down in a comfortable place where you will not be disturbed. Read it slowly, have someone read it to you, or record it and play it back.

> Welcome. Find a comfortable position, either sitting up in a chair or lying on your back on the floor or on a bed. Take a moment to get comfortable. And become aware of your body now ... You may wish to stretch various parts of your body ... your arms, your legs, your neck, or your back ... just to heighten your awareness of your body. And now begin to take a few deeper, longer and slower breaths ... inhaling through your nose and exhaling through your mouth, if you are able to do that. And continue the long, slow rhythmic breathing ...
>
> And now, let's take a few moments to focus upon, and appreciate, your body. Feel the air coming in and out of your lungs, bringing you life energy. And be aware that your lungs go on breathing, even when you are not aware of it ... breathing in and out, all day long, all night long, even when you sleep ... breathing in oxygen, breathing in fresh pure air, breathing out the waste products, cleansing and restoring the entire body, a constant inflow and outflow of air ... just like the ocean, like the tide coming in and going out. And so just now, send a beautiful and radiant white light and love to your lungs and realize that ever since you took your first breath your lungs have been there for you. No matter what we do, they still keep breathing in and out, all day long. And now become aware of your diaphragm,

that muscle below your lungs that goes up and down and continually allows your lungs to breathe ... and send light and love to your diaphragm.

And now become aware of your heart. Feel it and appreciate it. Your heart is a living miracle. It keeps beating ceaselessly, never asking for anything, a tireless muscle that continues to constantly serve you ... sending life-giving nutrients throughout your body to every cell. What a beautiful and powerful instrument! Day in and day out your heart has been beating. And so see your heart surrounded by white light and warmth, and say silently to yourself, "I love you and I appreciate you" to your heart.

And become aware now of your blood which is pumped through your heart. It is the river of life for your body. Millions upon millions of blood cells ... red corpuscles and white corpuscles ... anticoagulants and antibodies ... flowing through your bloodstream, fighting off disease, providing you with immunity and healing ... bringing oxygen from your lungs to every cell in your body ... all the way down to your toes and up into your hair. Feel that blood moving through your veins and arteries ... and surround all of those veins and arteries with white light. See it dancing in the bloodstream as if it were bringing joy and love to each cell.

And now become aware of your chest and your ribcage. You can feel it rising and falling with your breathing ... your ribcage which protects all of the organs in your body ... protects your heart and your lungs ... keeping them safe. So let yourself send love and light to those bones that make up your ribcage. And then become aware of your stomach and your intestines and your kidneys and your liver. All of the organs of your body that bring in food and digest it and provide the nutrients for your body ... balancing and purifying your blood ... your kidneys and your bladder. See your whole body from your neck down to your waist surrounded and filled with white light.

And then become aware of your legs ... your legs which allow you to walk and to run and to dance and to jump. They allow you to stand up in the world, to move forward and to run and to make yourself breathless with exhilaration. Allow yourself to appreciate your legs and to feel them surrounded with white light. And see all the muscles and bones in your legs filled with radiant white light ... and say to your legs, "I love you, legs, and I appreciate all the work that you've done." And then become aware of your feet. They let you stay balanced as you go through the world. They allow you to climb and to run ... and they support you every day ... and so thank your feet for being there and supporting you.

And then become aware of your arms. Your arms are miracles too. And your hands. Think of all the things you are able to do because of your hands and your arms. You can write and type ... you can reach out and touch things. You can pick things up and use them. You can bring food to your mouth. You can put things away that you don't want. You can scratch and itch, turn the pages of a book, cook food, drive your car, give someone a massage, tickle someone, defend yourself, or give someone a hug. You can reach out and make contact with your world and with others. So see your arms and your hands surrounded with light, and send them your love.

And then allow yourself to feel gratitude for having a body, one that you can use every day, to have the experiences you want to have, and that you need to grow and to learn from.

And then become aware of your spine, which allows you to stand up straight ... and it provides a structure for your whole body ... and it provides protection for your nerves that go from your brain down your spine and out to the rest of your body. See a golden light floating up your spine, from the base of your spine at your pelvis ... floating up your spine one vertebra at a time, moving up your spine, all the way up to your neck ... to the top of your spine where your skull connects ... and let that golden light flow up into your brain.

And then become aware of your vocal cords in your neck ... they allow you to speak, to be heard, to communicate, to be understood, and to sing and to chant and to pray, and to shout, and yell with delight and excitement ... to express your feelings and to cry and to share your deepest thoughts and your dreams.

And then become aware of the left side of your brain, the part of your brain that analyzes and computes, that solves problems and plans for the future, that calculates and reasons and deducts and inducts ... And just allow yourself to appreciate what your intellect does provide for you ... and see the left side of your brain totally filled with golden and white light ... and shimmering little stars, and see that white light cleanse and awaken and love and nurture that part of your brain ... and then let that light begin to flow across the bridge from the left side of your brain to the right side of your brain ... the part of your brain that allows you to feel, to have emotions, to be intuitive, to dream ... to daydream and to visualize, to create, and to talk to your higher wisdom ... the part of your brain that allows you to write poetry and to draw ... and to appreciate art and music. See that side of your brain filled with white and golden light.

Then sense that light flowing down the nerves into your eyes ... and see and feel your eyes filled with that light, and realize the beauty that your eyes allow you to perceive: The flowers and the sunsets and the beautiful people ... all the things that you've been able to appreciate through your eyes.

And then become aware of your nose. It allows you to smell and to breathe and to taste ... all the wonderful tastes and smells in your life ... the beautiful fragrances of flowers and the essence of all the foods that you love to eat.

Now become aware of your ears ... they allow you to hear music, to listen to the wind, the sound of the surf at the ocean, and the singing of birds ... and to listen to the words "I love you" ... and to be in discussions and to listen to the ideas of another, to allow understanding to come forward.

And now feel every part of yourself from head to toe surrounded and filled with your own love and your own light ... And now take a moment and allow yourself to apologize to your body for anything you may have done to it ... for the times you weren't kind to it and for the times that you didn't care for it with love ... the times that you didn't listen to it ... for the times that you put too much food or alcohol or drugs into it ... for the times you were too busy to eat, too busy to exercise ... too busy for a massage or for a hot bath ... and for all the times your body wanted to be hugged or touched and you held back.

And once again feel your body ... and see yourself surrounded with light ... And now let that light begin to expand out from your body ... out into the world ... expanding out, filling the space around you.

And now begin to bring that light slowly back into yourself, very slowly, back into your body, into yourself ... and experience yourself here, now, full of light and full of love and appreciation for your body ... And when you're ready, perhaps you begin to let yourself stretch and feel the awareness and aliveness back in your body ... And when you're ready, you can slowly begin to sit up and readjust to being in the room and just let your eyes open, taking as much time as you need to make that transition.

8

Care for Your Mind by Caring for Your Body

B ecause the mind and body are interactively connected, taking care of the body is a way to strengthen mental health and self-esteem. Stated more emphatically, we can't expect to feel our best psychologically if we neglect our physical health. The good news is that (1) we now know how to optimize physical health, and (2) the investment of time, money, and effort required to accomplish this is not excessive. Physical health is like a three-legged stool, which topples if one of the legs is missing. The three legs of physical health are sleep, exercise, and nutrition.

Sleep

Although we spend a third of our lives in bed, sleep hasn't been seriously studied until recently. Sleep deprivation has become much more common, and we now know that insufficient sleep adversely affects mood, immunity, insulin resistance, levels of stress hormones, heart disease rates, energy levels, weight gain, memory, traffic accidents, and work and athletic performance.

Two factors comprise good sleep (Dement and Vaughan 1999). The first is the amount of sleep. Most adults need more than eight hours per night to feel and function at their best, but the typical adult gets less than seven and carries an accumulated sleep debt that exceeds twenty-four hours. A single good night's sleep will not pay off this sleep debt but will instead tend to make one feel drowsier the next day. You can determine your sleep needs by sleeping as long as you can each night over a period of several weeks until your sleep levels off at a consistent number of hours. This is the amount you need. Alternatively, assume that you need 8.25 hours of sleep per night. If you feel drowsy after getting this amount of sleep for several weeks, add twenty minutes or more.

The second factor necessary for good sleep is regularity. The brain regulates sleep rhythms, which weaken as we age. To keep sleep cycles regular, we need regular wake-up and retiring times. Adults typically shortchange themselves during the week and then try to make up the lost hours over the weekend. This disrupts sleep cycles and tends to promote insomnia and daytime drowsiness. Try to retire and rise at the same time each day, even on weekends, varying these times by no more than an hour from one day to another. If possible, avoid nighttime shift work, which is associated with higher rates of a number of diseases and shorter life spans. If your shift times vary, see if your supervisor will agree to let you move from earlier to later shifts (the brain handles staying up later better than it does retiring earlier). Stay on each new shift for as long as possible, to allow the brain to adjust to the change. For example, you might try to start with the 9:00 A.M. to 5:00 P.M. shift, and then move to the 5:00 P.M. to 1:00 A.M. shift, and finally move to the 1:00 A.M. to 9:00 A.M. shift. Ideally, you would maintain each shift for weeks or even months.

Aids to a good night's sleep include the following:

- **Get a medical exam** to rule out and/or diagnose conditions that can impair sleep or cause daytime fatigue, including thyroid disorders, diabetes, anemia, bruxism, hyperventilation, gastroesophageal reflux, or sleep disorders. If sleep apnea (or another sleep disorder) is suspected, ask your doctor for an overnight sleep study in order to evaluate it. Apnea causes daytime drowsiness, depression, and a host of other disease symptoms, but it can be effectively treated.

- **Treat clinical depression, anxiety, or problem anger,** all of which can degrade sleep. If you have recurring nightmares, try describing the nightmare in your journal. Then write down a different ending—any one you wish. Mentally rehearse the new dream with its new ending for a few minutes daily.

- **Create an optimal sleep climate.** Completely darken the room—cover any clock radios that may be emitting light and ensure that the morning sun does not come through windows. Minimize sounds (use earplugs or white noise) and movements (keep pets outside of the bedroom). Maintain a peaceful, soothing sleep environment in your bedroom by using it only for activities that are relaxing. Pay bills, watch television, study, and talk on the phone in other areas of your home instead of in your bedroom.

- **If you seem to benefit from naps, take them consistently during the early afternoon.** This is the siesta time in some cultures, when the body temperature drops. The recommended nap time is from 15 to 120 minutes, with great individual variability. If napping seems to make it difficult for you to fall asleep at night, then try avoiding naps in order to consolidate nighttime sleep.

- **Lose weight through exercise.** Losing just a few pounds reduces snoring, which can also reduce daytime headaches. Try exercising before dinner, in order to allow your body time to relax before bed. Exercise is perhaps the most effective way to shorten the amount of time needed to fall asleep, to improve sleep quality and sleep duration, and to reduce nighttime awakenings, even in the elderly.

- **Reduce or eliminate caffeine, nicotine, and alcohol.** These disrupt people's sleep, even when they don't realize it. Try to avoid these for at least four to six hours before retiring.

- **Wind down before retiring.** Try eating a light snack of carbohydrates with a tryptophan source (such as crackers with cheese, sweetened yogurt, turkey, bananas, oats, eggs, or a few almonds). Eat dinner early and keep it light, with a small serving of protein to prevent night-time hunger. Write down your worries and/or plan your next day at least an hour before retiring. Turn lamps to their lowest setting or use nightlights, to allow your brain to wind down (strong lights signal the brain to stay awake). Shut off the phone and television at least an hour before you go to bed, and then retire when you are sleepy, not when the clock says to. A warm bath an hour or two before bedtime promotes sleep.

- **Don't rely on sleeping pills.** Instead, use sleep hygiene and skills that reduce stress and anxiety, which improve sleep without side effects. Effective sleep programs promote sleeping regular hours, getting out of bed if you don't fall asleep within thirty minutes, doing something that is not stimulating until you are ready to try going to bed again, reducing the intake of liquids in the evening, practicing relaxation and abdominal breathing, and reducing catastrophic thoughts (such as "It's awful that I can't fall asleep"). As one guru taught, "When tired, take sleep." And remember that even an extra twenty minutes of sleep per night can significantly improve mood and performance.

Exercise

Dozens of studies have found a link between exercise and self-esteem (Spence, Poon, and Dyck 1997). Physical activity also sharpens thinking, improves the mood, raises energy levels, fights aging, and helps to prevent a host of medical diseases. The current federal exercise guidelines call for at least thirty minutes of exercise most, or preferably all, days. If one is trying to stay or become fairly lean, then the recommended amount increases to sixty to ninety minutes. These amounts are considerably greater than those recommended previously because the country has become so sedentary. Getting this amount of exercise is less difficult than it might seem at first. For example, one might engage in moderate aerobic exercise most days, such as walking (or swimming, jogging, biking, stair stepping, or tai chi) for at least thirty minutes. If you can, supplement this activity with exercises that build muscular strength and endurance three or more times a week. For example, in ten to fifteen minutes, one could do ten repetitions each of several exercises, such as weight lifting (enough weight to cause moderate fatigue), resistance band exercises, push-ups, or abdominal crunches. Stretching and flexibility exercises, such as gentle yoga, can be added, or alternated with resistance exercises.

Below are a few tips that can help you get started:

- The greatest fitness gains are typically seen in people who were previously sedentary. However, it's important for you to have reasonable expectations, start very slowly, and progress very gradually. You will be unlikely to continue if you overdo it. Take a few months to work up to your desired exercise levels. Aim to feel refreshed after you exercise, not exhausted or sore.

- If you are over forty years of age or have health concerns, such as diabetes or risk factors for heart disease, discuss your plans with your physician and undergo a physical exam.

- If you can't do all your exercise at once, add small amounts of exercise to your daily routine. Try getting away from your desk for ten-minute energy walks every ninety minutes or so. Take the stairs instead of the elevator. Or park your car farther away from the office than you usually do so that you can walk more.

While you watch television, you might do light resistance or flexibility exercises.

• Don't be discouraged if you gain a little muscle weight as you begin to exercise. Muscle weighs more than fat, but it burns calories much more efficiently than fat, so you will become leaner as you continue to exercise.

Nutrition

Along with inactivity, overeating is associated with our growing obesity epidemic and a number of diseases. But intelligent eating can improve mood, performance, and energy levels while helping us to stay lean.

The nation's dietary guidelines are consistent with abundant research linking nutrition to health. The following are the daily intake guidelines given by the USDA (2005) for healthy eating, assuming a total intake of 2,000 calories per day (the approximate amount considered healthy for most adults):

Fruits. *A total of 2 cups of fresh, frozen, or canned fruit*

Vegetables. *A total of 2½ cups of cut-up raw or cooked vegetables (Beans such as black, garbanzo, soy/tofu, or lentils can be counted here or in the meat group, but not in both.)*

Grains. *A total of 6 one-ounce equivalents, where a one-ounce equivalent is a slice of bread; ¼ to ½ cup dry cereal; ½ cup cooked rice, pasta, or cereal; or 3 cups popcorn*

Lean meats and beans. *A total of 5½ one-ounce equivalents, where a one-ounce equivalent is 1 ounce of cooked fish, poultry, lean meats; an egg; ¼ cup cooked dry beans or soy/tofu; 1 tablespoon of peanut butter; or ½ ounce of nuts or seeds*

Milk. *A total of 3 cups, where a one-cup equivalent is 1 cup low-fat or fat-free milk or yogurt; 1½ ounces of low-fat or fat-free natural cheese; or 2 ounces of low-fat or fat-free processed cheese*

Oils. *A total of 6 one-teaspoon equivalents, where a teaspoon equivalent is 1 teaspoon vegetable oil or soft margarine; 1 tablespoon of low-fat mayonnaise; or 2 tablespoons of light salad dressing*

A quick look at these guidelines reveals that an optimal eating plan derives most of its calories from plant sources. Plant foods provide fiber, vitamins, minerals, antioxidants, and phytochemicals that are all vital for good mental and physical health. Seek a wide variety of fruits and vegetables in different colors. As a general rule, the darker and richer the colors, the more nutrients the plant contains. So look for red, orange, yellow, and dark-green plant foods. Most or all of the grains in a healthy diet will be from whole-grain sources (such as oatmeal, whole wheat, bulgur, quinoa, brown rice, or popcorn). Aim to consume some nuts, seeds, and/or legumes most or all days. Although nuts and seeds can be high in calories, they contain a number of important nutrients, including healthy fats, and have been found to come with a number of health benefits. A one-ounce equivalent of nuts is about a small handful.

Needed unsaturated fats are found in fish and vegetable oils, with olive and canola oils being among the most beneficial plant oils. Try to avoid "trans" or hydrogenated fats, found in commercially prepared snacks, baked goods, baking mixes, stick margarine, and fried fast foods; also try to avoid excessive amounts of animal fats.

If we focus on obtaining the needed nutrients each day, we will worry less about what we should avoid, in part because we'll be less hungry. The fiber in plant foods, for example, tends to keep blood sugar levels steady and thus helps to moderate hunger. Consume foods that are high in water volume and/or fiber and low in fat, including fruits, vegetables, soups, whole grains, legumes, and low-fat dairy products. These high-weight, low energy density foods fill us on fewer calories. Dry snacks (pretzels, chips, cookies, crackers, and dried fruits, for example), french fries, bagels, cheese, bacon, and cream sauces are best used sparingly.

The following are some other helpful pointers:

- Try not to dip below about 1,600 calories per day. To do so would likely deprive you of needed nutrients, while slowing your metabolism and hastening weight gain, especially if you are not exercising.

- Drink plenty of fluids throughout the day, since this can help to reduce appetite and fatigue. Fluid can be obtained from the food and beverages we consume. You will want to restrict your intake of sweetened drinks, however, since drinking a single can of soda per day can account for gaining about sixteen pounds each year.

- Successful dieters have been found to eat breakfast and four or five smaller meals daily. They also tend to follow meal plans that are low in fat and calories, with most of their calories coming from complex carbohydrates (in other words, from unrefined plant sources). Minimize your intake of refined carbohydrates, such as candy, sugary sodas, high-fructose corn syrup, and white bread.

- Prepare your own meals and avoid restaurant foods as much as possible. This will help you control portion size, added fats, and added salt and sugar. If you order dessert, consider sharing it. Since the portion sizes at restaurants are usually several times larger than the portion sizes eaten at home, take some of your restaurant meal home.

- If you choose to lose weight, do so very gradually (perhaps one-half to two pounds per week), combining moderate exercise with carefully selected food choices and portion sizes.

How well do these guidelines work? Researchers have studied Okinawans, who are known for living long and healthy lives. The Okinawans' diet generally adheres to the guidelines we've discussed. On average, they consume seven servings of vegetables, three servings of fruit, and seven servings of whole grains per day. Seventy-two percent of their diet by weight comes from plant foods, 11 percent from fish, and only 3 percent from animal products (meat, poultry, and eggs). Overall, the diet is low in fat, salt, and sugar and is high in complex carbohydrates. They practice the rule of stopping eating when they are 80 percent sated, averaging about 1,800 calories per day, compared to about 2,500 calories consumed by Americans. The elderly people there also remain physically and mentally active and take naps. Unfortunately, it is thought that the health benefits of living on the island of Okinawa will erode as fast foods and other aspects of modern living are assimilated into their culture.

9

Develop Your Character and Spirituality

S elf-esteem, much like happiness, is cultivated from within, and the process benefits from consistent nourishment and constructive effort. It's a common belief that we are born with an upward reach, a desire to grow and progress toward our potential, and that we feel better about ourselves as we do so. This chapter will explore pathways to inner enrichment, drawing upon themes that are common across diverse cultures and spiritual traditions.

Developing Character

Character is one's moral, or inner, strength. There is nothing complicated or exclusive about moral living; it is not the province of any particular group. Moral behavior is simply behavior that is good, decent, and in the best interest of self and others. People with character strive to remain true to their own standards despite pressure. Morality involves both avoiding what is wrong and doing what is right for its own sake, even when wrong is done to us. At great risk to his career and safety, Japanese consul to Lithuania, Chiune Sugihara, defied his government, feverishly writing visas that saved more than 6,000 Jews from the Nazis. After the war, he was imprisoned by the Russians and dismissed from his government's service. A samurai who had been taught to help those in need, Sugihara and his wife had decided to follow their consciences simply because that was the right thing to do. Viktor Frankl (1959) observed that many prisoners in the World War II concentration camps became like animals, yet some demonstrated the highest character imaginable. Each person, he said, can choose the better course.

Morality is not imposed, it is freely chosen. We might summarize what we know about character:

- People today are less concerned with living ethically compared to people in previous decades. Studies suggest that many people today lie on a regular basis and cheat at work.

- Moral regrets can negatively affect our mental health. That is, the quality of our inner experience changes when we betray values that are important to us.

- Committing to ethical living builds self-esteem and related traits, such as peace of conscience, self-respect, self-trust, self-confidence, satisfaction with life, and wholesome pride and dignity. Indeed the word "integrity" suggests a sense of wholeness.

- Virtuous people have less to fear, being freer of condemnation from others and from self.

They are more likely to be valued by others, especially if they are not judgmental of others. In the peace of conscience that comes with being virtuous, we can see our own wisdom minds reflected.

- Carl Jung stated that there can be no morality without freedom. We might reverse this statement and say that without morality there is little inner freedom. That is, without morality, we are prone to become attached to aggression, ego, greed, or appetites.

- At the root of morality are love and the desire to live in harmony with self and others. Love for self, concern for all beings, and the desire to make the world a better place leads to moral behavior. As Buddha taught, we will not harm others if we truly love ourselves, because harming others destroys our own peace. One can strive for personal goals without stepping on others—instead, we can try to lift others as we climb.

- Character requires consistent practice. As Chambers (1963) said, we can't take a moral holiday and still be moral.

Dean John Burt (personal communication) has reasoned that self-esteem requires ethical self-approval. It is difficult to approve of oneself if one hurts the self or others, so the prudent course is to avoid hurting and to seek the good for self and others. Further, neutral behavior brings the risk of labeling oneself as insignificant, so it is also prudent to actively strive to do good.

REFLECTIONS

We might ponder the following reflections, drawn from various cultures:

"Happiness does not consist in pastimes and amusements, but in virtuous activities." (Aristotle)

"Nothing can bring you peace but yourself. Nothing can bring you peace but triumph of principles." (Ralph Waldo Emerson)

"All God's creatures are his family; and he is the most beloved of God who does most good to God's creatures." (Muhammad)

"Character cannot be developed in ease and quiet. Only through experience of trial and suffering can the soul be strengthened, ambition inspired, and success achieved." (Helen Keller)

"Silver and gold are not the only coin; virtue too passes current all over the world." (Euripides)

"Human dignity ... can be achieved only in the field of ethics, and ethical achievement is measured by the degree in which our actions are governed by compassion and love, not by greed and aggressiveness." (Arnold J. Toynbee)

"Character is power." (Booker T. Washington)

"Oh what a tangled web we weave, when first we practice to deceive." (Sir Walter Scott)

"As long as I listen to my conscience I feel peaceful."
(Tim Blanchette)

Then you might consider the following questions, suggested by Thomas G. Plante (2004):

- Would you trust a business that had cheated you or lied to you?

- Do you tell "little white lies"?

- Would someone trust you after catching you in a lie?

- When is it necessary to compromise your integrity by lying? Would the person you're talking with be irrevocably damaged by an honest but tactful response to a question like "How does this look?" Or might the person who hears "I don't think that color flatters you" actually be more likely to trust your opinion in the future? Is it wiser in the long run to say "I stopped for a drink after work" (even though this might require an apology or explanation) than to lie and say "I was working late"?

- Do you trust yourself more when you do the right thing?

- Would you feel more inner satisfaction if you were consistently honest and did the right thing more often?

Exercise: The Kind Character Inventory

Certain common virtues are valued in virtually all societies and cultures. Moral development does not require the imposition of somebody else's values, but committing to those that we desire for ourselves because they are in the best interest of ourselves and others. Below is a list of commonly prized character strengths. Please complete this exercise dispassionately and without judging or condemning yourself.

1. Rate the degree to which you demonstrate each of the following character strengths from 0 to 10, where 0 means that you never demonstrate that strength at all and 10 means that you demonstrate that strength as well as anyone possibly could.

    _____ Honesty, truthfulness

    _____ Fairness

    _____ Respect of self

    _____ Respect of others

    _____ Justice

    _____ Tolerance, acceptance of differences

    _____ Courtesy

    _____ Service, altruism, generosity, elevating others

    _____ Honor, integrity

    _____ Punctuality (not keeping people waiting)

    _____ Loyalty, faithfulness

    _____ Ability to keep confidences

_____ Responsibility, dependability, trustworthiness (doing what is expected, what one is paid for, what one commits to)

_____ Courage

_____ Temperance (avoiding excesses in spending, gambling, eating, substance use, and so on)

_____ Environmental stewardship (recycling, conserving energy, limiting gasoline use, not littering, and so on)

_____ Care, kindness, thoughtfulness, consideration (considering impact of one's own behaviors on others)

_____ Modesty

_____ Humility

_____ Sexual decency (respecting partner, not exploiting or manipulating partner)

_____ Tact

_____ Harmlessness (not hurting others verbally or physically)

2. Circle each strength that you would wish to further develop.

3. Select two or three of the circled strengths that are most important to you. Then consider the following:

    Think of times when you were younger when you acted with integrity in situations involving these strengths. How did it feel?

Is your conscience now at peace regarding these strengths? If not, what would it take for you to achieve this peace?

4. Pick one of these character strengths and practice it over the next month. Commit to a plan. Practice this plan now in small ways so that you will be able to apply the character strength later under pressure.

5. Commit to the cultivation of additional character strengths, one at a time, in a similar way over the ensuing months.

Sharon Salzberg (2004) suggests honoring at least five basic precepts that might help us in gradually cultivating character strengths: refraining from lying (and using harsh speech), stealing (taking what is not given), killing or physical violence, using sexual energy in a way that causes harm, and intoxication (which renders us less able to control our actions).

Why do you hasten to remove anything which hurts your eye, while if something affects your soul, you postpone the cure until next year?

—Horace

Forgiving Self

The human condition presents a dilemma. We certainly feel better about ourselves when we live honorably and constructively. Yet we are human, which means that we are imperfect and inevitably make choices that are *not* honorable and constructive, sometimes doing things that hurt ourselves and others. In other words, our behaviors fall short of our ideals, and we make mistakes. If we attach to the missteps and conclude that we are hopelessly bad, our self-esteem and motivation to improve will suffer. Forgiving ourselves allows us a way out of this dilemma. Forgiving helps us to begin again joyfully despite our errors. Formerly, forgiveness was only considered important for spiritual well-being. However, recent research has shown that forgiving also results in diverse psychological and medical benefits. As you'll see in the following story, it can also have other benefits.

An elderly woman was returning to her van after shopping in the supermarket. As she approached her van, she saw four young men in it. Putting down her bags, she pulled a gun out of her purse and shouted, "I have a gun and I know how to use it." The young men quickly ran away. The woman got into the van but was shaking so badly that she couldn't insert the key into the ignition. Finally she calmed down enough to realize that she was in the wrong van. She got out and located her own van, parked nearby. She felt so bad that she drove to the police station and explained to the sergeant what she had done, apologizing profusely. The sergeant laughed and said, "That's okay, lady. You see those four young men over there? They just reported that they were accosted by a crazy gray-haired lady with a gun." The men dropped the charges. Sometimes, when we are just trying to get through life, struggling with its many confusing events and choices, we do the wrong thing. When this happens, forgiveness is beneficial.

WHAT IS FORGIVENESS?

Forgiveness means choosing to release resentment, anger, bitterness, hatred, and the desire to punish or avenge past offenses or wrongdoings. We can choose to forgive even when the offender does not deserve it.

Why do we do this? We forgive in order to dissolve our attachments to the past. Although an offense in our life might be long past, we often continue to battle the memory, which becomes a burden that weighs us down and prevents us from moving on. In the battle, we might be judging the wrongdoer for his or her "badness." We might be planning how we will get even or punish the offender. In forgiving, we step back from the battle. We free ourselves from the past, realizing that punishing, getting even, and judging do not heal. We stop insisting that the past be changed before we can again be happy, and we instead take responsibility for our present happiness. Paradoxically, in releasing the burden, we gain greater control of our lives.

Forgiving ourselves is just as important. If we can't come to terms with our own past wrongdoings, then our present experience becomes colored by shame—we see only the bad in ourselves. Such a self-concept saps the joy in our life's journey: there is no pleasure in unremitting guilt, self-loathing, or self-condemnation. Shame drains the energy we need to respond fully to others' needs. It is difficult to be sensitive to others' needs when we are focused on, and weakened by, our own unhealed wounds. We might think that constantly reliving the offense will prevent its recurrence, but in reality such replaying tends to diminish the capacity to live well.

Forgiving is not any of the following:

Condoning, excusing, or viewing the offense with casual complacency. In fact, when forgiving we take responsibility for improving ourselves and ensuring that the offense is not repeated.

Completely forgetting. Indeed, we want to preserve the lesson, but release the painful emotions.

Minimizing the damage that has been done. Instead, understanding the damage caused helps us to avoid repeating the offense.

Allowing offenses to continue. We cannot control other people's choices about their behavior. However, we can ensure that our own behavior changes. Indeed, we must do our best to make sure that we are harmless if we are to be happy.

Reconciling with or trusting the offender. When the wrongdoer is someone else, it may not be wise to reconcile if that person is likely to repeat the offense. However, reconciliation with and restoring trust in self is the goal after forgiving oneself.

THE BASIC STEPS OF FORGIVING SELF

Confucius said, "The more a man knows, the more he forgives." The following steps can help us to apply forgiveness to ourselves.

1. **Acknowledge the hurt that has been done to others and self by your behavior.** Sit with this idea and consider it in a kind, nonjudgmental way. Realistically assign responsibility for the offense. For example, a rape victim might blame herself completely because she thinks she was careless. A more realistic view is that the perpetrator was responsible for the crime, not the victim.

2. **Make amends as much as possible** (apologize, restore what was taken, and so on).

3. **Commit to live as honorably and constructively as you can, using what you now know.** This is all anyone can do. Realize that the future is still uncharted, and wrong turns can be expected.

4. **Make friends with guilt.** Guilt is a beautiful emotion that alerts us when something is wrong so that we may achieve peace with our conscience. Without conscience there would be no morality. So we can greet guilt cordially and with acceptance, just as we do all other emotions. After we respond to guilt, it has done its job and we can release it. Hayes (2005, 193) reminds us that we do not come with owner's manuals, so "respectfully decline your mind's invitation to beat yourself up for not knowing what was in the owner's manual you were never given ... You did the best you could at the time. You know more now."

5. **Judge behaviors, not core worth.** Remember that who you are at the core is bigger than your isolated decisions, bad choices, or wrong turns. A bad decision made one day or during a particular period is not the essence of who you are. A wrong turn doesn't mean we can't correct course and get back on track, nor does it mean that the core value is lost. Wrong turns don't define us or invalidate our core worth; they only point out areas to improve. We can accept mistakes as a part of our history and then move on in life. In forgiving ourselves, we recognize that we have the potential to change and to reclaim the goodness within us.

6. **Be willing to constantly feel imperfect.** Being imperfect, as all of us are, does not negate worth or forever disqualify us from trying anew. To be human is to err. It is unkind to condemn oneself for doing so. If we have stumbled off a path we value, it is only destructive to think, "You see, I knew I couldn't do it." This is not who you are; it is just a thought. It would be much better to accept disappointment and think, "Imperfect people stumble; I can get up and back on the path."

7. **Maintain the beginner's mind.** Thinking "I'm no good" attaches us to the past in a negative and narrow way. The beginner's mind keeps us open to who we are and what we may become. This view is not limited by what we did in the past; instead it motivates us to reengage with life in a productive way.

8. **Continue doing good.** Reflect upon the good things you've done in the past. Keep doing these things.

9. **Let the offender off the hook.** It is said that no one in his or her right mind will intentionally do a hurtful thing. One who does wrong might be suffering or ignorant of how to get his or her needs met constructively. If you have done your best to rectify the offense and correct your course so you'll be less likely to do it again, let yourself off the hook.

BE A GOOD PARENT TO YOURSELF

Some are too easy on themselves, viewing extremely hurtful actions casually. Others (perhaps including you, since you've chosen to read this book) are too hard on themselves. But regardless of our backgrounds, we can learn to become good parents to ourselves. One way to do this is to learn how to care for ourselves when we are feeling pain over something that happened in the past. Consider the internal dialogue a parent might have about a beloved daughter who feels bad about a past mistake.

Question: Why did she do that?

Answer: Because she's imperfect.

Question: Does she deserve forgiveness?

Answer:	Not really. She is guilty of the offense.
Question:	Does she deserve punishment?
Answer:	Yes, if justice is to be served.
Question:	Do I trust her completely to be perfect and never again make a mistake?
Answer:	No, but knowing her I'm pretty sure she'll try her best to avoid repeating this mistake.
Question:	Do I want her to suffer continuously for the mistake?
Answer:	No.
Question:	Why not?
Answer:	Because I love her and want her to progress and be happy. Lingering guilt will only hold her back.
Question:	So what's the best thing to do?
Answer:	Instead of condemning her and fixating on her faults, I'll reclaim her and free her to learn and grow. In short, I forgive her.

Now go through this dialogue again. Only this time, replace the words "she" and "her" with "I," "me," and "myself," as appropriate.

GUILT AND SELF-DESTRUCTIVE PRIDE

A certain kind of self-defeating pride can keep us attached to guilt. Below are the thoughts of self-defeating pride and their rejoinders:

"Other people do those kinds of things, but I'm better than others and I should have known better."

Why should you have known better? Are you expecting to be more perfect than you are? Perhaps you could accept that you're imperfect, just like everyone else. Maybe you could stop judging and condemning yourself and instead focus on improving your skills or behavior. Maybe you could stop comparing yourself to others and simply focus on what you are presently choosing and doing. Let ego and judgment dissolve in favor of loving-kindness.

"If I try hard enough I'll be perfect and measure up to my idealized image."

If you try very hard, you'll likely approach your potential, but you'll always fall short of perfection. This is what humans do. Release shame, which causes us to say "I am no good and will never improve." Yes, a mistake means we are fallible. Nevertheless, we are still infinitely worthwhile and capable of overcoming our mistakes and changing course.

"Someone who doesn't meet his or her goals perfectly doesn't deserve to feel good. That person should be punished."

Again, one who falls short of one's ideal is fallible, which doesn't ever disqualify that person from trying again and feeling good. We can feel satisfaction from knowing that we are striving to do the right thing in the best way that we know. Everyone already suffers from having shortcomings. We can learn to hold this suffering with compassion, instead of judgment, punishment, and condemnation. Compassion is a much stronger motivator.

FORGIVING IS DIFFICULT

It can be difficult to let go of an offense, because the problem-solving mind wants to fix and get rid of problems. This approach works wonderfully for concrete, external problems such as a flat tire. It does not usually work for internal problems such as the memory of an event in our past. Sometimes one must first heal before letting go of old offenses that have affected us internally, and some feel that divine assistance facilitates this process. Those who are spiritually inclined might find comfort in the story below, which I call the "Parable of the Broken Microscope Slides" (Shupe 2006). One Sunday, in a small country church in Maine, the pastor gathered the children around him and told them this tale:

> When I was a young grade-school boy in Colorado, my teacher said, "Take your coats with you to recess. You won't be allowed to return to get them." I thought, no problem, I won't be cold. Once outside, however, I was getting *very* cold. I was really afraid to go back to the room, but reasoned it was better to risk my teacher's wrath than to freeze to death, and I was clearly freezing to death. So I snuck back into the classroom. Back in the closet where the coats were hung I grabbed my coat and pulled it down. Along with the coat came a box of brand new microscope slides crashing down and breaking into pieces all over the floor. I quickly ran back outside.
>
> Once we came inside, the teacher said, "Somebody knows who broke those slides. Can anyone tell me who it was?" I just hung my head and kept my mouth shut for the rest of the day. Returning home, I felt really bad and my mother knew something was wrong, but I said nothing. Finally, I could stand it no longer and blurted out the story to her. She said, "It's

okay. Just tell your teacher what happened and offer to pay for the slides." At the time I was only getting twenty-five cents a week for allowance and figured I'd be thirty-seven by the time I finished paying. But I went in and told the teacher: "I was just freezing and tried to get my coat and I didn't mean for the slides to break, and was too embarrassed to tell you, but I will pay my whole allowance of twenty-five cents a week."

At that point the teacher stretched the truth considerably. He said, "I noticed that only two slides were broken, so you can pay fifty cents and that will cover the damage." I had exactly fifty cents in the bank and so was extremely relieved.

The moral of the story: God is in the business of loving and forgiving. Don't ever assume that you've done something so bad that God won't forgive and love you. Don't hide from God when you make a mistake, but turn to Him in your weakness to experience His healing love and mercy.

The thought that God doesn't forgive people because of mistakes is just a thought.

Exercise: Forgiving Self

This activity combines mindfulness and ACT skills that have been introduced in previous chapters. Remember that trying to erase a memory doesn't usually work very well. Instead we can try the mindfulness method of letting the memory into our awareness completely and holding it with compassion.

1. Identify a previous wrong turn (decision, behavior, or misstep) that still troubles you.

2. Make a list of the resulting thoughts (such as "I'm no good" and "That was such a dumb thing to do"). Do this without judging or emotionally reacting. Whatever you think and feel is okay. Fully accept the suffering that you caused to yourself and others.

3. Reduce each thought to a single word or two that describes the associated feeling. This process might look like this:

Thought	Feeling
"I'm no good."	Bad
"I'm so disappointed in myself."	Disappointed
"I fear that this will be discovered."	Embarrassed
"I lost my innocence."	Shame
"I lost my sense of playfulness."	Numb
"I hurt someone."	Sad
"I lost my family's confidence."	Grief

4. Recall the Milk, Milk, Milk exercise in chapter 3. In this exercise you fully experienced milk in your mind, and then you repeated the word "milk" aloud as fast as you could for forty-five seconds. In doing this, people usually notice that the meaning of the word falls away and the word simply becomes a sound. Now, look at the first feeling word on your list from step 3 and welcome it into your awareness, holding it with complete acceptance and kindness. Repeat the word aloud as fast as you can for forty-five seconds.

5. Repeat this process for the other feeling words. Don't judge the feelings or try to get rid of them.

6. When you have finished, then calm yourself. With a soft and open heart, sit with the memory that has bothered you, holding it and any associated feelings, thoughts, or sensations compassionately, in the vast loving-kindness of the wisdom mind. Breathe into the memory, and let it settle.

7. When you are ready, breathe out and release the memory, letting awareness of the memory dissolve as you exhale.

8. Form the intention to forgive. Say the following in your mind:

> *For each time I have failed to meet my expectations and harmed myself or others I offer forgiveness. I seek to heal so that I will be harmless to others, happy, and useful.*
>
> *May I be whole. May I be forgiven. May I release the pain. May I progress. May anyone I've hurt be whole and happy. May he or she progress.*

Wisdom tells me I am nothing. Love tells me I am everything.

—Nisargadatta Maharaj

Forgiving Others

It is stressful to remain angry and bitter about past offenses committed by others. Such feelings cover the true self. As is the case with forgiving the self, forgiving others frees us from carrying a heavy load and permits us to experience our core self more favorably. Forgiving is the kind thing to do for oneself; it is also the kind thing to do for others. Sometimes, though not always, forgiving helps the offender change. During the Los Angeles race riots of 1992, Reginald Denny was dragged from the truck he was driving, beaten, and severely injured. Although he was angry, he explained that he truly loved the offender and embraced his parents. The offender's mother said that Denny's response began the process of softening her son's anger.

Although forgiving an offender might not change that person, it is an act of strength that changes the forgiver's experience. The Dalai Lama has explained that Tibetan monks who have been tortured by the Chinese don't typically suffer posttraumatic stress disorder. This is because the monks see the offenders as people who are suffering, and they respond with compassion for them and for themselves.

Exercise: The Candle of Forgiveness

The following powerful strategy (Eifert, McKay, and Forsyth 2006) can aid in the difficult process of forgiving. The authors explain that we can't develop compassion if we are running away from our experience. Try spending at least fifteen minutes each day doing this exercise.

Light a candle, then sit comfortably in the meditator's position (feet flat on floor, spine comfortably erect, upper body relaxed, hands resting in the lap). Allow your eyes to simply watch the candle flame.

As you watch the flicker of the candle flame, bring your attention to the gentle rising and falling of your breath in your chest and chest and belly. Like ocean waves coming in and out, your breath is always there. Notice its rhythm in your body. Notice each breath. Focus on each inhale ... and each exhale. Notice the changing patterns of sensations in your belly as you breathe in, and as you breathe out. Take a few minutes to feel the physical sensations as you inhale and exhale.

Step 1: Acknowledge the Wrong and Hurt Underneath the Anger

Now allow your awareness to shift to a recent situation where you became angry. See if you can allow yourself to visualize the scene fully. What happened? Who else was there? Watch the candle as you acknowledge the anger situation unfolding in your mind's eye. Focus on your breathing as you watch the situation unfold. With each slow breath, see if you can slow the anger situation down, like a slow-motion movie. As you do, bring your attention to any sensations of discomfort that show up. As best you can, bring an attitude of generous allowing and gentle acceptance to your experience right now. See if you can make room for the pain and hurt you had then and that you may be reliving now. Soften to it ... as you breathe in ... and out ... in and out. Don't try to fight what you experience. Open up to all of it: the hurt, pain, sadness, regret, loss, and resentment. Allow yourself to become more aware of your hurt and painful emotions [such as any feelings of fear, abandonment, loneliness, inadequacy, or being devalued by self or others], and simply acknowledge the hurt you experienced and the hurt you may have caused. Don't blame. Simply acknowledge and become aware of your experience.

Step 2: Separate Hurtful Actions from Your Hurt and Its Source

Visualize the person who hurt you. As you begin to visualize that person, allow them to drift over to the candle and become the candle. Focus on the candle as the person who hurt you, and remember what happened. As you focus on the candle, notice what your mind, the language machine, is doing, and the sensations that come up. You might see your mind passing judgment ... blaming ... and lingering over feelings of sadness ... bitterness ... resentment. As these and other thoughts and sensations come into your awareness, simply label them—"There is judgment ... blame ... tension ... resentment"—and allow them to be. Bring a gentle and kind awareness to your pain and hurt as you breathe in ... and out ... in ... and out ... slowly, and deeply.

Next, create some space between the actions that made you feel hurt and angry and the person who committed them. If it helps, you can visualize the action that hurt you as the flame and the person who committed the hurt as the candlestick. Notice the difference between the flame and the candle. The flame is not the candlestick. The actions of the person who hurt you are not the same as the person who committed them. As you breathe in and out, give yourself time to connect with this difference. Bring each hurtful action into the flame, one by one, and notice it, label it, and then see the difference between the hurtful action and the person who committed it. Visualize what was done, not who did it.

Then, after you spend some time noticing each action, allow it to disappear up into the heat leaving the candle flame. Keep watching any tension, discomfort, anger, hurt, or whatever else your body may be doing. Make room for what you experience as you return your attention to your body and your breathing. Don't change or fix anything.

Step 3: Bring Compassionate Witness to Your Hurt

Next, bring your attention back to the human being symbolized by the candle—the perpetrator of wrongs against you. Notice how he or she is also a person who is vulnerable to harm, just like you. At a basic human level, the two of you are not that different. See if you can allow yourself to take his or her perspective as a compassionate witness—see what life might be like through that person's eyes. Connect with his or her hardships, losses, missed opportunities, poor choices, faults and failings, hurts and sadness, hopes and dreams.

Without condoning that person's actions, see if you can connect with his or her humanity and imperfections as you connect with your own humanity and imperfections, hardships, loss, pain, and suffering. As a compassionate witness to this other human being, see if you can connect more deeply with that person as another human being. Notice the offender's thoughts and feelings, knowing that you've also experienced similar types of thoughts and feelings. What might it be like to have lived the life of the person who offended you? As best you can, bring an attitude of generous allowing and gentle acceptance to what you experience now.

Step 4: Extend Forgiveness, Let Go, and Move On

Now see if you can bring into awareness what your life would be like if you let go of all the negative energy you are holding on to—your grievances, grudges, bitterness, and anger. Connect with the reasons behind why you want to be free from anger and the desire for revenge. Allow yourself to visualize an alternative future full of the things you have missed out on or given up by not offering forgiveness. See if you can connect with your future without [forgetting] about what has happened in the past, and without carrying the weight of bitterness, anger, and resentment toward the person who hurt you.

Allow yourself to take the courageous step forward in your life of letting go of your anger and resentment. Perhaps you can feel the burden and weight of past hurts and unresolved anger begin to lift from your shoulders. Take time to really connect with this relief as you imagine yourself separating from the resentment and bitterness you have carried for so long. Allow all of it to drift away with each out breath, and with each in breath welcome peace and forgiveness. Continue to breathe in ... and out. Slowly. Deeply.

When you're ready, bring into your awareness how you have needed other people's forgiveness in the past. Imagine extending that forgiveness to the person who hurt or offended you. What could you say to that person now? As you think about this, notice any discomfort showing up and how your mind is reacting. If the thought "The person doesn't deserve that" shows up, just notice that thought and gently let it go. Return your focus to your breathing as you remind yourself that kind and gentle acts of forgiveness are for *you*, not for others. Imagine the weight of the burden being lifted from you as you choose to give forgiveness. Allow yourself to connect with the sense of healing and control that comes along with this. As you give the powerful gift of forgiveness, notice some budding feelings of softness where before there was only hardness, hurt, and pain.

Embrace this moment of peace as you return to the image of the person who offended you. Gently extend your hands as you say, "In forgiving you, I forgive myself. In letting go of my anger toward you, I bring peace to myself. I invite peace and compassion into my life and into my hurt and pain. I choose to let go of this burden that I have been carrying for so long." Repeat these phrases slowly as you extend forgiveness.

Stay with and simply observe and label whatever thoughts and feelings come up as you extend this act of forgiveness. Sense the emotional relief that comes when the burden of a grudge is melting away. See if you can notice the peace and feeling of inner strength that comes about as you extend compassion and forgiveness in this moment. Then, when you're ready, bring awareness back into the room, to your body, and the flicker of the candle flame. Finish this exercise by blowing out the candle as a symbolic gesture of your commitment to forgive and let go, and your readiness to move on with your life.

Sometimes we cling to resentment, thinking that it will protect us from being hurt again. If releasing resentment is difficult, accept that difficulty without judging. Each attempt is useful. Additional healing may need to precede forgiveness. Continue to extend healing compassion to your hurts.

Spiritual Contemplation

Just as people who feel bonded to loving adults tend to feel a sense of inner security, people who feel close to God often report feeling a deeper sense of security and an affirmation of their worth. This seems to be supported by research in recent decades indicating that spirituality and religious involvement offer wide-ranging psychological and physical benefits— including less anxiety, depression, suicide, substance use, and physical disease; greater life satisfaction; improved marital satisfaction; and extended longevity.

For example, using Gallup Poll data on adults age eighteen to ninety-eight, J. R. Peacock and M. M. Poloma (1999) investigated relationships between life satisfaction and religious and spiritual variables. Previous research (Pollner 1989) had found that one's relationship with God was a stronger correlate of life satisfaction than race, income, age, marital status, and church attendance. Peacock and Poloma found that perceived closeness to God was the strongest correlate of life satisfaction across the life course, followed by prayer experience (feeling God's presence, inspiration, or peace during prayer), church or synagogue membership, church or synagogue attendance, and practicing various types of prayer.

CLOSENESS TO GOD

The word *contemplation* derives from two Latin roots: *con*, meaning "with," and *templus*, meaning "a space to meditate." Thus, spiritual contemplation implies making room in our lives to experience God's presence. An intention shared by most spiritual traditions is to help individuals draw closer to God, who, depending upon one's tradition, might be addressed as the One, One Being, the Beloved, Creative Power, Compassionate One, Allah, Providence, Source of All Being, Lord, the Absolute, Adonai (Supreme Being), Shekkinah (Indwelling One), Master of the Universe, Higher Power, Father, Abba (in Aramaic this is an intimate form of address used by children for their father), or various other titles.

In many spiritual traditions, the purposes of spiritual contemplation are described as detaching from thought and opening ourselves to God's nearness; trusting in God; resting and refreshing in God's loving presence; sensing divine union, communion, and connection; experiencing an intimate, loving relationship with God; and finding the sacred in ourselves and in everyday moments. These purposes are suggested by the following reflections:

"Heaven means to be one with God." (Confucius)

"When my father and my mother forsake me, then the Lord will take me up." (Psalms 27:10)

"When you have succeeded in enshrining God within your heart, you will see Him everywhere." (Swami Sivananda)

"The highest aim of man: the knowledge of God." (Moses Maimonides)

"God is at home. We are the ones who have gone out for a walk." (Meister Eckhart)

"Come unto me, all ye that labour and are heavy laden, and I will give you rest." (Matthew 11:28)

"[When Peter] exclaimed, 'Lord, if it be thou, bid me come unto thee on the water.' Christ's answer to him was as it always is every time: 'Come.'" (Jeffrey R. Holland)

"As you move one step toward the One, the One moves ten steps closer to you." (Sacred tradition attributed to Muhammad)

"Whenever we find mention of God's greatness, we also find mention of His humility. He is great enough that a single human being can be as significant to Him as an entire universe." (Talmud)

"Whether you love God or love a human being, if you love enough you will come into the presence of Love itself." (Rumi)

"What we love we become. Those who call on God with sincerity will find the living presence of that God within themselves." (Kabir Edmund Helminski)

"The Lord is my shepherd ... He leadeth me beside the still waters ..." (Psalms 23:1–2)

"That they all may be one; as thou, Father, art in me, and I in thee, that they also may be one in us." (John 17:21)

"Man does not need a tour of the world's cathedrals to come in contact with the deity. He just needs to look within. To do this one must sit still." (Albert Schweitzer)

"My presence shall go with thee and I will give thee rest." (Exodus 31:14–15)

"In giving ourselves to God, we discover who we really are." (Anonymous)

"Know ye not ... that the Spirit of God dwelleth in you?" (1 Corinthians 3:16)

Exercise: Spiritual Contemplation

God speaks in the silence of the heart ... and we listen.

—Mother Teresa

This meditation typically takes about twenty to thirty minutes. Find a place where you won't be disturbed, and begin. (You might consider prerecording this script or having someone read it aloud to you.)

1. Prepare your body and mind. You might wish to stretch, walk, or bathe before starting. As well as you can, release anger, hatred, fear, and any other negative attachments.

2. Sit in the meditator's posture (feet flat on the floor, back comfortably erect, hands resting in the lap). Remember the attitudes of mindfulness, especially compassion, acceptance, patience, nonjudgment, and good humor.

3. Close your eyes.

4. Peacefully watch your breath. Let your mind and body settle in your breath. Allow the agitated water of the soul to also settle and become clear ... quiet ... still. Anchor in your breathing, getting beneath the thoughts of the ordinary mind. Don't judge the wandering mind. When thoughts arise (such as "I don't think I'm doing this right"; "I do not deserve to do this"; "This feels really good—I don't want it to end"; and "What if this doesn't work?") just recognize these as thoughts, and bring your attention back to resting in your breath.

    If you find it helpful, say silently or aloud several times a soothing word (such as "love," "near," "peace," "calm," "one," or "Abba") or phrase (such as "divine presence," "closer to Thee," or "love of God"). Repeating the word or phrase for a while helps to quiet the mind.

5. Let a half smile form on your face and notice how that feels. Then let that smile and feeling of contentment spread throughout your body.

6. And now consider God's infinite, tender loving-kindness and mercy. Spend a few moments pondering all the divine gifts that inspire feelings of gratitude ... anything great or small that blesses your life or helps you ... anything beautiful and good. Notice what comes to awareness. (Perhaps you think of the smiles of loved ones ... a drink of clear, cold water or clear water to bathe in ... the fragrance of mowed grass or flowers ... the breeze on your skin ... clouds ... a bed to sleep in ... what the body can do—move, enjoy sexual intimacy, speak ... tasty food ... toothpaste.) As you notice the creative power hidden in all of these, perhaps you also recognize the creative power hidden in you ... that you belong ... a valued part of the larger whole ... a universe where all things are interconnected. And we refer to this creative power in the universe in an intimate way, calling God *our* Lord, helper, protector, comforter ... and appreciate that the master of creation cares for, and is near to, each created individual. Meditate on this love for a few moments. Allow feelings of gratitude and happiness to rest in your body.

7. Take a slightly deeper breath and let it go. And now turn inwardly toward God ... aware of God's loving-kindness ... receptive to God's presence. You might see yourself picking up your concerns and approaching God ... reaching toward ... with a soft and open heart ... feeling God's presence nearer. Whatever you feel is okay, whether it is comfort ... security ... warmth ... contentment ... light ... or just quiet, simple stillness ... In your own way open to

that presence ... Release, relax, and rest in God's loving presence ... feeling at home ... peaceful, healing communion ... with the wonder of the beginner's mind ... not trying to make anything happen, but patiently receptive to whatever way you experience divine presence in the quiet stillness of your heart.

8. Rest in that quiet peacefulness and security for several minutes, breathing gently.

9. Be aware that you can remember divine presence throughout the day, and that you can repeat this meditation. When you are ready, slowly open your eyes.

OTHER WAYS TO DRAW CLOSER TO GOD

Spiritual contemplation is but one way to experience closeness to God. Praying is another complementary path. Prayer can be ritualistic (as in reading from a book of prayers or reciting a memorized prayer) or expressed from the heart, and it can come in the form of adoration or praise, gratitude, conversation (speaking in your own language and words and talking over problems, plans, or concerns), and petition (asking for assistance, guidance in decisions, or forgiveness). Reading sacred writings, attending worship services, doing acts of service (sometimes called "love in action"), and living in a holy way are also ways of opening ourselves to God's nearness. Mother Teresa taught that holiness is a simple duty for everyone; one can be holy in any state or position in life. In so doing, we can choose to release habits that are self-destructive or harmful to others and choose to go about doing good in a variety of ways (such as rendering small acts of kindness to family members). Father Thomas Keating (1992), who writes extensively on contemplation, says that repentance is changing the direction in which one is looking for happiness.

The spirit is the true self, not that physical figure which can be pointed out by your finger.

—Cicero

10

Look Ahead

Optimism, which correlates with self-esteem, lets us look forward to a satisfying life. Life satisfaction is built upon emotional intelligence skills (such as healing and taking care of ourselves emotionally), persisting in doing what is working, personal growth, and cultivating meaning and purpose, among other things. This chapter will explore three remaining processes related to self-esteem and life satisfaction: personality development, cultivating meaning and purpose, and relapse prevention.

Personality Development: Opening to What We May Become

Personality development becomes enjoyable when the secure foundations of unconditional worth and unconditional love are in place. But there is a driven, joyless quality in trying to improve when these foundation stones are lacking. So it is best to learn the skills in this chapter last, after you have worked to boost your feeling of self-worth, and self-love.

We call personality development a process because it is ongoing, never fully completed. The journey can be traveled with a kind and playful attitude. Think about the enjoyable aspects of people you know—friends, relatives, neighbors, children, coworkers, or famous people. We don't change overnight, and we wouldn't wish to become just like somebody else, but we can trust ourselves to cultivate our latent personality traits in a way that is unique to ourselves. Consider the below list of traits that are generally valued in people:

Appreciative	Playful
Determined, resolute	Warm
Open to new experiences	Sincere
Sense of wonder/delight/awe	Comfortable with the full range of emotions
Flexible (not rigid; adaptable, willing to bend)	Grateful
Gentle	Courteous
Enthusiastic	Attuned to others, attentive, interested
Friendly, inviting	Courageous (persists despite fear)
Vulnerable (does anyone enjoy those who think they're perfect?)	Respectful
Strong	Thoughtful
Hardworking	Safe, comfortable to be with

Calm	Self-reliant (not needy)
Articulate	Encouraging
Organized	Steady
Humble	Adventurous
Patient	Kind
Poised, graceful	Tactful
Fun loving	Upbeat (doesn't dwell on negatives)
Independent, self-motivated	Curious
Forgiving	

Can you think of other traits that you would add? If you were to select five personality traits to cultivate, just for fun, which would they be? Circle these. Then simply be open to cultivating these traits in your life. You might meditate from time to time on how your life would be different if these traits were more fully developed. For example, if you'd like to cultivate courtesy, you might reflect upon how saying thank you, letting drivers go in front of you, doing nice things for others, or smiling at salesclerks would make you and others feel. The wonderful thing is that personality growth can continue even as our aging bodies decline.

Man's only legitimate end in life is to finish God's work—to bring to full growth the capacities and talents implanted in us.

—Eric Hoffer

Meaning and Purpose

Self-esteem correlates highly with one's sense of meaning and purpose. The famous concentration camp survivor Viktor Frankl (1959) observed that knowing one's life has meaning and purpose confers a calm inner strength that enables people to endure great suffering. Frankl explained that the concentration camps caused some to sink to depravity, but others rose to greater heights of character and selfless service. Survivor's pride, felt by resilient people who have lived through great suffering, includes individuals (1) discovering that they have an existing inner strength that is greater than adversity, and (2) knowing that their lives still have meaning and purpose. Meaning and purpose derive from discovering and developing character and personality strengths. They also derive from the use of these strengths to benefit others, which Aristotle described as a pathway to happiness.

Studies have shown that defining success primarily in material ways leads to poorer psychological adjustment. However, a common theme across cultures is that those who think of others and aim to better the world discover greater happiness and awareness of their inner worth. People who understand this early in life are fortunate. In the Japanese culture, *kigatsuku* is the inner spirit that helps us see the needs of others and help without being told. The gifted teacher Chieko Okazaki relates that when she was a child her mother would say, "I'm looking for a kigatsuku girl to help me with the dishes." Pretty soon she learned to see what was needed and then help without being asked. Traveling widely today doing public service, she might pick up trash in a public bathroom, which she feels privileged to use, explaining that helping is everybody's job.

How might we make the world a better place? There are many ways. When someone asked Mother Teresa how he might help her, she simply said, "Come and see." We can simply observe what needs to be done, and do it as best we can. This might mean providing physical help (such as cleaning or giving a ride) or giving a smile, a listening ear, or encouragement. Simple expressions of help can be given to family, friends, coworkers, or strangers. Or, if we have the means, we might donate time or money to a worthwhile cause (such as a soup kitchen, Mothers Against Drunk Driving, Habitat for Humanity, or a political campaign). Further, you can think of your job as a way to contribute. For example, one janitor might view his job as simply cleaning and getting rid of trash. Another might view it as creating an environment that helps educators teach and a generation of children to learn.

Another way to make the world better is to beautify or improve our environment for the sake of others. This could involve artistic expression (such as painting or poetry), inventing, sprucing up your home or workplace, or picking up litter on your walking path. Additionally, you can think about what it would be like to be in another person's shoes and see how your behaviors affect that person. Plante (2004) reminds us that the hotel housekeeper cleans up others' messes and might be ignored by the guests. Perhaps she would appreciate receiving a simple greeting from the guests she cleans for. A salesclerk might be tired after a long day of dealing with demanding customers. An empathic smile or a word of thanks for her service might go a long way.

S. C. Hayes (2005; Eifert, McKay, and Forsyth 2006) reminds us that we all carry burdens—perhaps memories, partially healed wounds, worries, self-doubts, or fears. Rather than trying to ignore, deny, or hide these, you can think of them as passengers on the bus that you are driving through life. You compassionately acknowledge that they are aboard, but you needn't listen to every demand to stop, take a detour, or let them drive. In this way we can move ahead purposefully in life, even with these imperfections. Remember that you are driving, not being driven. Choose a pace that is comfortable.

You can't do everything, and you can't do it all at once. But you can experience the security and satisfaction of doing what you *can* do.

There is no greater satisfaction for a just and well-meaning person than the knowledge that he has devoted his best energies to the service of the good cause.

—Albert Einstein

Relapse Prevention

We have explored many useful skills for building self-esteem. As is the case with learning to play an instrument or a sport, we improve our skills with practice. These skills can soften the blows of difficult life situations, helping to preserve self-esteem in the face of adversity.

The final skill, relapse prevention, will allow you to anticipate and develop a coping plan for a difficult situation that could threaten your self-esteem. This is how well-trained athletes, warriors, firefighters, and other individuals anticipating stressful situations prepare—they rehearse what they will think and do before, during, and after encountering a distressing or challenging event. The principle is that we are less likely to be thrown by a difficult situation if we are prepared for it.

Exercise: Stress Inoculation

1. Identify a difficult situation that could undermine your self-esteem. This might be something like performing poorly on an important task, failing to meet important personal goals, or encountering a situation that could lead to rejection, mistreatment, or criticism.

2. Place a check by any statement that might be useful in coping with such a difficult situation.

Before

☐ This could be difficult and challenging. I'll take a breath and do the best I can.

☐ If I stay calm and do my best there's a good chance that I'll do well.

☐ No matter what happens, I'll still be a worthwhile person.

☐ Nobody's perfect. Relax and do what you can.

☐ This is an opportunity to stretch myself. I view it as an opportunity.

☐ I'm not afraid to risk and fall short, because I know that my worth comes from within, not from my performance.

☐ It will be fun to succeed. If I don't, it won't be the end of the world.

☐ I'll gain useful experience, even if I fall short of my goal.

☐ I'll focus on doing what I can and not worry about how things turn out.

- ☐ I'll aim for an excellent job, not perfection.

- ☐ I have as much right as anyone to try at this.

- ☐ I'll feel the satisfaction of giving this my best shot, and I won't worry too much about the outcome.

- ☐ I'll calmly size things up and then handle it as well as I know how. That's all anyone can ask of a person.

- ☐ Other statements: _____

During

- ☐ Stay calm and focus on the task. (Worries take us off task.)

- ☐ Easy does it—one step at a time.

- ☐ It's natural to feel fear, tension, and frustration. Whatever I feel is okay.

- ☐ It's too bad that things aren't more perfect, but it's not a catastrophe.

- ☐ Sometimes we just have days like this. Keep trucking.

- ☐ I accept that this is a difficult situation.

- ☐ Whatever happens, *I'll* be okay inside.

- ☐ Things needn't go perfectly.

- ☐ Remember to laugh. I may not be perfect, but I know that I'm still cool inside.

- ☐ Other statements: _____

After

If things went well:

- ☐ I did a good job. That went well.

☐ I tried my best and feel satisfied with the outcome.

☐ It's fun to tackle challenges and do well.

☐ Other statements: _____

If things didn't go well:

☐ I'm new at this. I'll try a different approach next time.

☐ That really was a difficult situation.

☐ That's water under the bridge.

☐ Everyone makes mistakes.

☐ Eventually I'll figure out how to succeed at this.

☐ Even though I'm disappointed, I'm still a worthwhile person.

☐ Despite the outcome, I have the right to learn from this and try again.

☐ Even though my skills weren't adequate for the task, I'm worthwhile as a person.

☐ Okay, now what? What's the best thing I can do now?

☐ This, too, will pass.

☐ I feel satisfaction in knowing that I tried my best.

☐ Okay, so I didn't do as well as I wanted to today. Perhaps with rest and more practice I can improve.

☐ Even if people judge me harshly, I can view the situation kindly.

☐ Because of this disappointment I will be especially compassionate toward myself.

☐ A slip isn't permanent.

□ Where there is life there is hope.

□ Years from now, will this really matter?

□ Other statements: _____

3. Write down several of your favorite statements from each category.

4. If you have read the preceding chapters, take this opportunity to review them to identify the principles and skills that are most useful for you. Then list what you will do before, during, and after the difficult situation. For example, before confronting the situation you might wish to exercise and do the body scan to calm down, and use your mastery and competence imagery to build confidence. During the difficult situation, you might wish to relax your body and breathe mindfully to remain calm, as you implement pre-planned strategies. Afterward, you might use your daily thought record and defusing skills, and your cognitive rehearsal, smile meditation, sitting with emotions, mindful mirror, and forgiving skills. (If you have not read the previous chapters, return to this step after doing so.)

5. Mentally rehearse what you will do and say before, during, and after confronting the difficult situation until you feel reasonably confident in your ability to cope with the situation. You can prepare for any difficult situation in this way.

Pursue some path, however narrow and crooked, in which you can walk with love and reverence.

—Henry David Thoreau

Recommended Resources

Books and Videos on Self-Esteem and Emotional Well-Being

Coopersmith, S. *The Antecedents of Self-Esteem*. San Francisco, CA: Freeman. A scholarly work about the causes and consequences of various levels of self-esteem.

Rosenberg, M. *Society and the Adolescent Self-Image*. Princeton, NJ: Princeton University Press. Another scholarly classic.

Hayes, S. C., with S. Smith. *Get Out of Your Mind and Into Your Life: The New Acceptance and Commitment Therapy*. Oakland, CA: New Harbinger Publications. This brilliant book explores the suffering we create in our minds by futilely trying to get rid of our histories. It teaches how to accept and then disengage from our inner battles, so that we can live a valued life. ACT has been found to reduce depression and anxiety and is useful for self-esteem issues.

Dr. Seuss. *Oh, The Places You'll Go.* New York: Random House. A clever, humorous treatise on human growth and fallibility. Written for children. Or is it?

Mother Teresa: A Film by Ann and Jeanette Petrie with a Narration by Richard Attenborough. Petrie Productions. Videocassette. San Francisco: Dorason Corp. A powerful object lesson in unconditional love. Although this is out of production, it is well worth the search.

Kevin Miller. 20/20 Downtown. Segment Two, 1/20/00. ABC News Home Video. Videocassette. A morbidly obese person nevertheless manages to preserve self-esteem.

Schiraldi, G. R. *The Self-Esteem Workbook.* Oakland, CA: New Harbinger Publications. Based on the successful "Stress and the Healthy Mind" course, University of Maryland. Contains detailed instructions for many effective skills.

Schiraldi, G. R. *The Post-Traumatic Stress Disorder Sourcebook: A Guide to Healing, Recovery and Growth.* Chicago: McGraw-Hill. When unresolved trauma undermines self-esteem. "The most user-friendly manual on PTSD I have ever seen. Must reading for victims, their families, and their therapists," according to Dr. George Everly, Executive Editor, *International Journal of Emergency Mental Health.*

Schiraldi, G. R., and M. H. Kerr. *The Anger Management Sourcebook.* Chicago: McGraw-Hill. Problem anger may be an expression of self-dislike. This book offers more practical skills on forgiving. "A must for those who are serious about managing their anger more effectively," according to Dr. R. J. Hedaya, Clinical Professor of Psychiatry, Georgetown University Hospital.

Schiraldi, G. R. *World War II Survivors: Lessons in Resilience.* Ellicott City, MD: Chevron. Extraordinary survivors describe the strengths that enabled them to function under extreme duress, preserve sanity, and return to lead productive lives. Self-esteem is an important component of resilience.

Schiraldi, G. R. *Conquer Anxiety, Worry and Nervous Fatigue: A Guide to Greater Peace.* Ellicott City, MD: Chevron. Anxiety and self-esteem are highly correlated, from hyperventilation to worrisome thoughts. "The best book for anxiety we've ever seen," said the staff at the Sidran Foundation.

Schiraldi, G. R. *Facts to Relax By: A Guide to Relaxation and Stress Reduction.* Provo, UT: Utah Valley Regional Medical Center. A range of traditional techniques and resources. (Utah Valley RMC, IHC University, 1134 North 500 West, Suite 204, Provo, UT 84604, tel. 801-357-7176)

Seligman, M. E. P. *The Optimistic Child.* New York: Houghton Mifflin. Using cognitive therapy to immunize children at risk for depression by building resilience. See Penn Resiliency Project (www.ppc.sas.upenn.edu/prpsum.htm) to learn more.

Seligman, M. E. P. *Authentic Happiness.* New York: Free Press. Happiness and self-esteem overlap in many ways, including the signature strengths discussed here.

Frankl, V. *Man's Search for Meaning.* Boston: Beacon. The classic work on discovering meaning in one's life out of suffering, written by the Holocaust survivor who founded logotherapy.

Ashe, A., and A. Ramparsad. *Days of Grace: A Memoir.* New York: Ballantine. Despite fighting prejudice and AIDS contracted during heart surgery, Arthur Ashe retained his dignity and optimism.

Opdyke, I. G., with J. Armstrong. *In My Hands: Memories of a Holocaust Rescuer.* New York: Anchor. A young Catholic girl in Poland risked her life to save Jews during WWII. Despite incredible hardship, she remained softhearted and optimistic.

Marx, J. *Season of Life.* New York: Simon & Schuster. Inspired by Viktor Frankl, former NFL star Joe Ehrmann now teaches highly successful young athletes that manhood is not found in athletic prowess, sexual exploitation, and materialism, but in love and meaning.

Eyre, L., and R. Eyre. *Twelve Children's Stories for Teaching Children Joy.* Salt Lake City, UT: Homebase. Includes clever instructions for appreciating unique differences.

Burns, D. *Feeling Good.* New York: Signet. A practical book on replacing the thinking distortions that cause depression and undermine self-esteem.

Books and Videos on Physical Health

Flow Motion: The Simplified T'ai Chi Workout. Video by C. J. McPhee and D. Ross, Tai Chi Video Productions (Lightworks Audio & Video, Los Angeles, 800-795-8273, or Collage Video, 800-433-6769). A gentle way to utilize the mind-body connection, lower blood pressure, and improve fitness.

Christensen, A. *Easy Does It Yoga*. New York: Fireside. Instructions for gentle postures for the aged, injured, or inactive. Many are useful for anyone and can be done at one's desk to relax and increase energy and flexibility.

Jacobs, G. D. *Say Good Night to Insomnia: A Drug-Free Program Developed at Harvard Medical School*. New York: Owl. Practical ways to improve sleep quality and quantity.

USDA. 2005. *Dietary Guidelines for Americans 2005*. See www.mypyramid.gov for personalized interactive nutritional information.

Books on Spiritual Contemplation and Meditation

Kabat-Zinn, J. *Full Catastrophe Living*. New York: Bantam Dell. Perhaps the best book on mindfulness meditation, a practice that has been found to reduce a host of medical and psychological symptoms.

Gefen, N. F. *Discovering Jewish Meditation: Instruction and Guidance for Learning an Ancient Spiritual Practice*. Woodstock, VT: Jewish Lights. In a warm and readable style, it provides practical instruction for lay readers.

Kaplan, A. *Jewish Meditation: A Practical Guide*. New York: Schocken. Rich in insights.

Dalai Lama, and H. C. Cutler. *The Art of Happiness: A Handbook for Living*. New York: Riverhead. Profound insights on self-esteem and compassion.

Hanh, T. N. *Peace Is Every Step*. New York: Bantam. Peaceful monk's practical ways to cultivate inner peace, joy, serenity, and balance.

Douglas-Klotz, N. *The Sufi Book of Life: 99 Pathways of the Heart for the Modern Dervish*. New York: Penguin Compass. Sufi meditation with a light touch.

Keating, T. *Open Mind, Open Heart: The Contemplative Dimension of the Gospel*. New York: Continuum. Father Keating provides a Christian perspective.

Books and Videos on Couple and Family Skills

Markman, H., S. Stanley, and S. L. Blumberg. *Fighting for Your Marriage: Positive Steps for Preventing Divorce and Preserving a Lasting Love*. San Francisco: Jossey-Bass. Based on solid research, this book provides practical advice on everything from conflict resolution to increasing fun.

Prevention and Relationship Enhancement Program [PREP]: Resources for a Loving Relationship. Denver, CO. (800-366-0166) *Fighting for Your Marriage* and other books. Four excellent videos to help develop communication skills, solve problems, and promote intimacy. The PREP approach is well researched and respected.

Lundberg, G., and J. Lundberg. *I Don't Have to Make Everything All Better*. New York: Viking Penguin. Treasure chest of methods for relating to people. Learn how to walk alongside people emotionally, rather than arguing or criticizing.

Lundberg, G., and J. Lundberg. *Married for Better, Not Worse: The Fourteen Secrets to a Happy Marriage*. New York:

Viking. Another down-to-earth treasure for creating a satisfying marriage.

Latham, G. I. *The Power of Positive Parenting: A Wonderful Way to Raise Children.* North Logan, UT: P&T Ink. Useful and thorough guide to steady, consistent, and peaceful parenting.

Garcia-Prats, C. M., and J. A. Garcia-Prats. *Good Families Don't Just Happen: What We Learned from Raising Our Ten Sons and How It Can Work for You.* Holbrook, MA: Adams Media Corporation. Principle-based skills, starting with respect between spouses.

Eyre, L., and R. Eyre. *Teaching Children Joy.* Salt Lake City, UT: Deseret. When we can teach it to children, then we have learned it.

Resources for Healing from Trauma

Trauma, which usually affects self-esteem, typically requires specially trained therapists.

Sidran Institute is a national nonprofit organization that helps people understand, recover from, and treat traumatic stress and related conditions. Provides information, treatment resources, reading lists, educational materials, and a caring ear at no charge to trauma survivors and family members. (To find a nearby trauma therapist, contact Sidran Institute, 200 East Joppa Road, Suite 207, Baltimore, MD 21286, tel. 410-825-8888, help@sidran.org, www.sidran.org.)

Intensive Trauma Therapy. Combines art therapy with videotaping and hypnosis in a very effective approach to individual treatment. Offers one- and two-week intensives. (314 Scott Ave., Morgantown, WV 26508, tel. 304-291-2912)

References

Albom, M. 1997. *Tuesdays with Morrie.* New York: Broadway.

Beck, A. 1976. *Cognitive Therapy and the Emotional Disorders.* New York: Meridian.

Beck, J. S. 1995. *Cognitive Therapy: Basics and Beyond.* New York: Guilford Press.

Brown, S. L., G. R. Schiraldi, and M. Wrobleski. 2003. Psychological strengths as correlates of happiness and health in college students. Paper presented at the Second International Positive Psychology Summit, Washington DC.

Chambers, O. 1963. *My Utmost for His Highest.* Uhrichsville, OH: Barbour.

Dement, W. C., and C. Vaughan. 1999. *The Promise of Sleep.* New York: Delacorte.

Eifert, G. H., M. McKay, and J. P. Forsyth. 2006. *ACT on Life Not on Anger: The New Acceptance and Commitment*

Therapy Guide to Problem Anger. Oakland, CA: New Harbinger Publications.

Ellis, A., and R. A. Harper. 1975. *A New Guide to Rational Living.* North Hollywood, CA: Wilshire.

Frankl, V. E. 1959. *Man's Search for Meaning: An Introduction to Logotherapy.* Boston: Beacon.

Gardner, H. 1993. *Frames of Mind: The Theory of Multiple Intelligences.* New York: Basic.

Gauthier, J., D. Pellerin, and P. Renaud. 1983. The enhancement of self-esteem: A comparison of two cognitive strategies. *Cognitive Therapy and Research* 7(5):389–98.

Goleman, D., ed. 2003. *Healing Emotions: Conversations with the Dalai Lama on Mindfulness, Emotions, and Health.* Boston: Shambhala.

Hayes, S. C., with S. Smith. 2005. *Get Out of Your Mind and Into Your Life: The New Acceptance and Commitment Therapy.* Oakland, CA: New Harbinger Publications.

Hayes, S. C., K. D. Strosahl, and K. G. Wilson. 1999. *ACT: An Experiential Approach to Behavior Change.* New York: Guilford Press.

Hinckley, G. B. 2000. *Standing for Something: Ten Neglected Virtues That Will Heal Our Hearts and Homes.* New York: Random House.

Hobfoll, S. E., and J. R. Leiberman. 1987. Personality and social resources in immediate and continued stress resistance among women. *Journal of Personality and Social Psychology* 52(1):18–26.

Hobfoll, S., and P. London. 1986. The relationship of self-concept and social support to emotional distress among women during war. *Journal of Social and Clinical Psychology* 4(2):189–203.

Jacobson, N., and A. Christensen. 1996. *Integrative Couple Therapy: Promoting Acceptance and Change.* New York: W. W. Norton and Company.

Kabat-Zinn, J. 1990. *Full Catastrophe Living.* New York: Bantam Dell.

———. 2005. *Coming to Our Senses: Healing Ourselves and the World Through Mindfulness.* New York: Hyperion.

Keating, T. 1992. *Invitation to Love: The Way of Christian Contemplation.* New York: Continuum.

Lee, H. J. 2002. Psychosocial variables associated with resilience among mother-daughter dyads. Doctoral diss., University of Maryland.

Lowry, R. J., ed. 1973. *Dominance, Self-Esteem, Self-Actualization: Germinal Papers of A. H. Maslow.* Monterey, CA: Brooks/Cole.

McQuaid, J. R., and P. E. Carmona. 2004. *Peaceful Mind: Using Mindfulness and Cognitive Behavioral Psychology to Overcome Depression.* Oakland, CA: New Harbinger Publications.

Miller, K. 2000. Interview by Anderson Cooper, *20/20 Downtown,* ABC (January 20).

Monson, T. 2006. True to the faith. *Ensign* 36(5):18–21.

Murray, W. H. 1951. *The Scottish Himalayan Expedition.* London: J. M. Dent and Sons.

Okazaki, C. N. 1993. *Lighten Up!* Salt Lake City, UT: Deseret.

Peacock, J. R., and M. M. Poloma. 1999. Religiosity and life satisfaction across the life course. *Social Indicators Research* 48:321–45.

Plante, T. G. 2004. *Do the Right Thing: Living Ethically in an Unethical World.* Oakland, CA: New Harbinger Publications.

Pollner, M. 1989. Divine relations, social relations, and well-being. *Journal of Health and Social Behavior* 30(1):46–53.

Rinpoche, S. 1993. *The Tibetan Book of Living and Dying.* New York: HarperCollins.

Rogers, C. R. 1987. *On Becoming a Person: A Therapist's View of Psychotherapy.* New York: Houghton Mifflin.

Salzberg, S. 2004. *Lovingkindness: The Revolutionary Art of Happiness.* Boston: Shambhala.

Schiraldi, G. R. 2001. *The Self-Esteem Workbook.* Oakland, CA: New Harbinger Publications.

Schiraldi, G. R., and S. L. Brown. 2001. Primary prevention for mental health: Results of an exploratory cognitive-behavioral college course. *Journal of Primary Prevention* 22(10):55–67.

Segal, Z. V., J. M. G. Williams, and J. D. Teasdale. 2002. *Mindfulness-Based Cognitive Therapy for Depression: A New Approach to Preventing Relapse.* New York: Guilford Press.

Shupe, P. C. 2006. Parable of the broken slides. Sermon delivered at Foreside Community Church, Falmouth, ME (March 26).

Spence, J., P. Poon, and P. Dyck. 1997. The effect of physical activity participation on self-concept: A meta analysis. *Journal of Sports Exercise Psychology* 19:S109.

Sprott, J. B., and A. N. Doob. 2000. Bad, sad, and rejected: The lives of aggressive children. *Canadian Journal of Criminology* 42(2):123–33.

USDA. 2005. *Dietary Guidelines for Americans 2005.* www .mypyramid.gov.

Warner, M., ed. 2004. *The Portable Walt Whitman.* New York: Penguin.

Zhang, L. 2005. Prediction of Chinese life satisfaction: Contribution of collective self-esteem. *International Journal of Psychology* 40(3):189–200.

Biographical Sketch

Glenn R. Schiraldi, Ph.D., has served on the stress management faculties at the Pentagon, the International Critical Incident Stress Foundation, and the University of Maryland, where he received the Outstanding Teaching Award in the College of Health and Human Performance. He is the author of various articles and books on human mental and physical health. His books on stress-related topics include *The Self-Esteem Workbook*; *The Post-Traumatic Stress Disorder Sourcebook*; *World War II Survivors: Lessons in Resilience*; *Conquer Anxiety, Worry, and Nervous Fatigue*; *The Anger Management Sourcebook*; *Hope and Help for Depression*; and *Facts to Relax By*. Glenn's writing excellence has been recognized by various scholarly and popular sources, including the *Washington Post*, the *American Journal of Health Promotion*, the *Mind/Body Health Review*, and the *International Stress and Tension Control Society Newsletter*.

While serving at the Pentagon, he helped to design and implement a series of prototype courses in stress management for the Department of the Army—including hostility/anger management and communication skills. He conducts resilience training for the prevention of post-traumatic stress disorder for the International Critical Incident Stress Foundation. Serving at the University of Maryland since 1980, he has pioneered a number of mind-body courses, which have taught skills to a wide range of adults to prevent stress-related mental and physical illness. He also served on the board of directors of the Depression and Related Affective Disorders Association, founded as a Johns Hopkins University Department of Psychiatry cooperative, and he presently serves on the editorial board of the *International Journal of Emergency Mental Health*, and on the ABC News Post-Traumatic Stress Disorder working group.

He is a graduate of the U.S. Military Academy at West Point, and holds graduate degrees from BYU (summa cum laude) and the University of Maryland.